Praise for *How to Be Busy*

"Finally, a book that addresses the realities of everyday life and the chaos that comes with it! *How to Be Busy* offers practical strategies to help us slow down and be more intentional about enjoying our lives."

—**Courtney Carver**, founder of Be More with Less; author of *Soulful Simplicity, Project 333*, and *Gentle*

"In a world cluttered with distractions, Rachelle Crawford shares a refreshing perspective on time management. *How to Be Busy* offers a relatable and practical approach to managing our time well during both the slower and busier seasons of life. It's a necessary read for anyone seeking to reclaim their time, energy, and attention for what truly matters."

—**Joshua Becker**, founder of Becoming Minimalist; author of *Things That Matter, The Minimalist Home*, and other books

"*How to Be Busy* offers a refreshing take on time management that values our pursuit of simplicity while honoring the reality that life can't always be (nor should it be) optimized. Crawford reminds us not to miss the beauty that's often hidden in our busyness—for it's how we navigate the seasons of our lives that determines what can add more to our plates than it takes away."

—**Christine Platt**, bestselling author of *The Afrominimalist's Guide to Living with Less*

"If you are too busy to read this book, then you are the person who needs it the most. Rachelle Crawford brings her lighthearted, shame-free humor to this topic that applies to many of us across the world.

She teaches us how to prioritize what matters the most in the seasons of life that feel overly full."

—**Denaye Barahona**, host of *Simple Families* podcast and author of *Simple Happy Parenting*

"Rachelle Crawford takes day-to-day small moments and turns them into witty, enlightening, often heartwarming stories that convey a powerful message. *How to Be Busy* is an important book for those of us navigating busy schedules while also desiring to live intentional and present lives. With grace and humor, Rachelle helps us learn what it means to be busy well."

—**Erica Layne**, author of *The Minimalist Way*

"In a world where busyness feels like the norm, Rachelle Crawford shows us that we don't have to live life in constant overdrive. Her practical, down-to-earth advice helps you rethink your daily hustle and release the things that no longer serve you. This book offers a refreshing approach to finding calm, and you'll come away with an actionable plan to create margin in your life. If you're ready to stop running on empty and start living with more intention, this is the guide you need."

—**Dawn Madsen**, host of *The Minimal Mom Podcast*

HOW TO BE
busy

HOW TO BE
busy

Unhurried Living Even
When Your Calendar Is Chaotic

Rachelle Crawford

BROADLEAF BOOKS
MINNEAPOLIS

HOW TO BE BUSY
Unhurried Living Even When Your Calendar Is Chaotic

30 29 28 27 26 25   2 3 4 5 6 7 8 9

Library of Congress Control Number: 2024033696 (print)

Cover image: © 2024 Getty Images; Check Mark Boxes/1341110852 by filo
Cover design: Broadleaf Books (Brynne Worley)

Print ISBN: 978-1-5064-9914-7
eBook ISBN: 978-1-5064-9915-4

To Paul, in all our seasons

To Paul, in all our seasons

Contents

CHAPTER 1 Over It 1

CHAPTER 2 Seasonal Living 13

CHAPTER 3 The Unhurried Life 25

CHAPTER 4 Be Mindful: The Art of Making and Keeping Margin 39

CHAPTER 5 Be Bored: The Practice of Under-Committing 51

CHAPTER 6 Be a Quitter: The Art of Walking Away 61

CHAPTER 7 Be Rude: The Art of Saying No 73

CHAPTER 8 Be Proactive: The Practice of Being Ready for Anything 87

CHAPTER 9 Be Prepared: The Importance of Creating a Busy Protocol 101

CHAPTER 10 Be Unreachable: The Importance of Eliminating Digital Distractions 111

CHAPTER 11 Be Uncluttered: The Practice of Owning Less Stuff 125

CHAPTER 12 Be on Your Mat: The Art of Undistracted Living 139

CONTENTS

CHAPTER 13   Be Present: The Art of Creating Meaningful
              Moments Out of Everyday Life   153

CHAPTER 14   Be Intentional: The Art of Deciding
              for Yourself   167

Resources   181

Acknowledgments   185

Notes   187

CHAPTER ONE

Over It

I took a shortcut through the produce section and had just pushed my shopping cart into the checkout line when my then-five-year-old hesitantly announced, "Mommy, I have to go potty."

Looking the other way so she wouldn't see my face, I rolled my eyes, inhaled, and then let out my most exasperated sigh. "Of course, you do," I mumbled to myself.

We had exactly zero time for her to pee. Isn't that how it always goes? Nobody loses a shoe, must pee *right now*, or shatters a drinking glass, dispensing shards of glass over two levels of kitchen surfaces, when they've got nowhere to be. Of course not. It's always going to happen when it's literally the last thing you have time for.

That's where I was at on this particular day as well: already cutting it close. We had barely enough time to grab the items we needed from the grocery store, make it across town to school, slide into the back of the pickup line to grab my older two, and then hightail it across town to wherever it was we had to be that day. Where, exactly? I can't even recall.

"You're just going to have to hold it," I said. Then I just stood there slowly shaking my head.

Yet it wasn't my sweet girl I was shaking my head at. It wasn't even the slow-moving shopper in front of me, nor the nonchalant checkout clerk, both of whom were moving way too slowly for my tight schedule. No, I was shaking my head at the words I had just spoken. I knew they were wrong before I even finished my sentence, but I was unable to pull them back in time.

This is what you'd call an *aha* moment. My life seems to be a series of them, divided not by decades but by points of no return. It would be far less painful to naturally mature at a slow and steady pace based on information we gain, books we read, or advice we receive. But change rarely occurs under comfortable circumstances. Something usually has to jar us awake. As Newton put it, "Objects in motion tend to stay in motion unless acted upon by an outside force."

Finding myself without enough time for my sweet young child to simply relieve herself was one of the many outside forces (however self-induced it was) that changed the way I think.

With that shake of the head, I backed my cart out of the checkout line, had her hop on the side of the grocery cart, and ran her to the bathroom. I vowed then and there never to let myself become this busy again.

Have I, though? Of course I have.

THE TROUBLE WITH BEING OVERLY BUSY

I wish I could tell you that story was a one-off. That it was a significant *aha* moment because it was such unusual and atypical behavior for me. But the reality is that I am accustomed to busyness—so much so that I never used to see it as something to change. It was a fixed truth in the doctrine of my very full life. I had gotten so used to the pace that I didn't even think about it. Being busy just came with the territory of being a living, breathing human.

As I write this, we are in the process of selling our home. After eighteen years in this sweet space, we are moving on. Prior to inspections, we as sellers were supposed to disclose any issues with the home to the potential buyers. But we couldn't think of a single thing to disclose. It's been a great home with no major issues. We did have a wicked bee's nest a few summers back, but that's long been resolved.

Yet as we pack up our belongings room by room, we're noticing there are in fact plenty of things we probably need to disclose. For example, the ice maker in our freezer stopped working years ago. We just started making ice cubes in trays. My son dented his bedroom door playing mini-hoop one afternoon. We placed a basketball wall decal over the heel-sized dent and called it good. And our coat closet doors won't shut after they're opened all the way. Instead of figuring out the issue and solving it (which would probably be super simple), we've just always reached up to the hinge and pushed down on the sliding doohickies. There were plenty of little issues, but we've lived with them for so long that we didn't even recognize them as issues. It's just the way things are around here.

The same thing can happen to our calendars. When busy is the only pace we know, we don't always recognize it as problematic. In fact, over time it can even start to feel somewhat comfortable. I used to think I *preferred* a busier life—so much so that I was constantly adding things to my calendar, planning outings with friends, and running unnecessary errands whenever I found empty space on my calendar. Downtime felt awkward and unproductive. And that was *before* having babies. Once I had kids, filling my calendar became effortless: playdates, work, volunteering, shopping for new stuff, running sick kids to the doctor, visiting Grandma, returning the stuff I had recently shopped for. Their nap schedules were my only saving grace. Once those babies outgrew naps and started school, all bets were off. My calendar just filled itself.

"Busyness" is pretty much the default factory setting of parenthood these days. It comes with the territory. It's like when you make an online purchase only to find yourself automatically opted into the seller's monthly subscription plan. Getting out of it takes more work than a federal tax audit. All you did was download an app or order your child an activity kit, and the next thing you know, they need a blood sample and lock of hair to unsubscribe you.

Most of the time we don't even know slowing down is an option. Instead, we double down, "try to find a better balance," learn to tolerate it, or manage to acclimate to our hectic schedules the same way we adjusted to the closet door that won't close properly.

A BRIEF HISTORY OF TIME

The concept of time management, at least the way we view it today, is a relatively modern phenomenon. Prior to the industrial revolution, people perceived time locally, as it pertained to the seasons and sunlight within their local community. There were no time zones or nationally regulated time. There didn't need to be.

All of that changed with the industrial revolution. Once regions became connected by train travel and telegraph communication, the contrast in local time became glaringly problematic. Train companies were each running on their own time-keeping systems, which made coordinated travel remarkably difficult. So in 1883, time zones were created.

Fast-forward to 1913, when Henry Ford developed the concept of the assembly line and time became even more quantifiable. Before the assembly line, it took 2 hours (and 12.5 total worker hours) to assemble just one car. After the development of the assembly line, however, it took just 15 minutes (and 1.5 worker hours) to assemble a single car.

So am I proposing we toss time zones to the wind and ditch the modern amenities brought about through vital leaps in engineering and innovation? Of course not. I could never go back to living in a time before air-conditioning, indoor plumbing, and modern medicine. I'd never make it.

What I want to point out is that it wasn't *always* like this. While the industrial revolution brought about advances we'd never want to live without, they're not without consequences. Everything comes with some sort of exchange. Take the invention of the light bulb. While it's certainly improved living conditions, it also left us with the opportunity for even longer working hours. (And thanks to my reading light, I'm able to read late into the night despite my need for sleep.) Even so, we're now compelled to clock in and out of our own lives like we're functioning on a one-person assembly line. Being as productive as possible has become our ultimate goal. Experiencing a day when we "didn't get anything done" leaves us feeling like a failure.

We've forgotten how to rest, play, and just do nothing. Even our leisure is exhausting. We take our limited time off—and then create a travel itinerary that leaves us needing a vacation from our vacation. I'm not pointing fingers here. Guilty as charged. (I'm not even sorry about it either. If you give me free rein to plan a two-week vacation, it's going to include a transatlantic flight and at least two different European countries. I can't help it.)

But even when we find ourselves with a free weekend or evening to spare, we struggle to *just be*. Instead of using our free time to fill back up, we keep pouring out in the name of getting caught up, keeping up, organizing our space, or accomplishing another home project. It's no wonder we're exhausted and overwhelmed all the time.

TIME REVOLUTION

One Wednesday morning, while navigating my overly cluttered and overly busy life, I tripped over the concept of minimalism, and everything changed. Long story short, I began decluttering our home, implementing minimalist principles, and becoming a more conscious consumer of material possessions.

Through the practice of owning less stuff, I started finding more time. It was incredible. Here I was donating sweaters I never wore and kitchen gadgets I hardly used, and in exchange I was finding free time and breathing room. It was glorious!

It didn't take long, however, before my attempt at an idealistic version of minimalism led me to crash and burn. You can read the full story of how this chronically messy gal adopted a grace-based form of minimalism in my book *Messy Minimalism*. Here's the Cliffs-Notes version:

- I found minimalism.
- I tried to implement some Insta-worthy version of minimalism that would guarantee my home always remained tidy and picture perfect.
- I crashed and burned because, obviously, that is neither a noble goal nor an attainable one.
- I almost quit minimalism entirely.
- I decided not to toss the baby out with the bath water but instead created a version of minimalism that fit my real life.
- Highlight: *Minimalism doesn't mean always tidy; it just means easily tidied.*

Bam. *Messy Minimalism* was born. What you get is a grace-based form of minimalism that will help you offload the excess by loading up on grace.

Prior to minimalism, my life was defined by clutter: a cluttered home, a cluttered mind, and a cluttered calendar. Busyness was my go-to coping method for avoiding the things that cluttered my head, home, and heart. I saw busyness as an achievement in and of itself. The more I could cram in and still remain standing at the end of the day, the better. I never once paused to assess where my time and energy were going, because all that mattered was that they were going somewhere.

Once I adopted a minimalist mindset, I began assuming the *opposite* was true. If being busy is sucking the life out of me, I thought, then having nowhere to go and nothing to do must be the solution. Minimalism initiated for me a much-needed time revolution. I now saw the antidote to an overly busy life as an abrupt halt to practically all activity. In my mind, over-busyness became an indication of my level of intentionality, or rather lack thereof.

So I spent the next six years or so in the constant pursuit of a slower pace. I pruned every possible facet of my life, perfecting my ability to say no to overcommitment. I had gone from wearing overly busy as a badge of honor to wielding my new superpower: the *unbusy* life.

It's funny, though. While it only took me a few months to realize that *minimalism* isn't a one-size-fits-all lifestyle, it took me *years* to draw the same conclusion about time management. I assumed if we were intentional and proactive enough with our calendar, we could keep busyness and chaos at bay, always and forever. So that's where I focused my energy.

Here's the kicker, though: That story about not having enough time for my little one to use the bathroom? That didn't occur prior to minimalism. I was well into living the simple, unbusy life I was so proud of. If it had occurred *prior* to simplifying my calendar, it would have made this book much easier to write. I'd be rocking a pretty stellar before-and-after story: my kids used to not even have time to pee and now they do. Can't you picture it? *Eradicating Busyness: How Decluttering Your Stuff and Your Calendar Means You'll Never Be Too Busy Again.* Join me on this journey and your kids can pee as well.

For some reason, however, with every passing year, I found it more and more difficult to keep the busy life at bay. In fact, I almost didn't even write this book. Because *that* was the kind of book I thought I should write. But abruptly after agreeing to write a book about managing our time well through the practice of simplicity, it happened *again*. I had the book contract in hand when my calendar took a sharp turn. Here was yet another wildly busy season that left me burnt out and asking myself, "What is happening?!" I kept wondering: *If I'm following the simple living recipe properly, why then do I keep finding myself in over my head?*

At the time, my middle schoolers' schedules had picked up, almost overnight, and we were just a couple months away from our move— only across town, nothing life-altering, but I still see why moving is listed as one of the top-five stressors a person can encounter. It was all fun and games when we were *oohing* and *ahhing* over our new home. But things got intense fast when it came time to actually pack up and move out of the only home our kids had ever known. We all felt overwhelmed, often. My husband Paul was absolutely swamped at work at the time as well, which left me carrying the lion's share of the family load. (Though he always helped tidy the kitchen after dinner each night. That man can clean a kitchen in less time than it takes for me to swap from my jeans to my pajama pants. It's a work of art, really.)

On top of all that, one day during that same busy season my accident-prone son wandered into the school nurse's office experiencing concussion symptoms after a run-in during gym class. This ended up leading to months of symptoms, appointments, and therapies, which took our already full calendar and absolutely decimated it. Of course those appointments naturally trumped my writing hours, leaving me staring down the barrel of a book contract I no longer felt qualified to write.

How could I possibly tackle the topic of time management when I was struggling just to keep my own head above water? I'd rather not write the book at all than feel like an overwhelmed hypocrite in the process. Each night, I'd crawl into bed looking for reprieve, only to lie awake second-guessing our move, worrying about my son's brain, and wondering if I should call my publisher to back out of this book deal.

The irony wasn't lost on me: I was just too busy to write a book about how to be unbusy.

BEING BUSY WELL

As any author will tell you, though, the book you end up writing often isn't the book you set out to write. This one includes a plot twist even I didn't see coming. I started to realize that the world didn't need another book about eliminating busyness, because busyness isn't always avoidable. While many of us compare our sense of being overwhelmed to the efficient strategies of business gurus and time-management experts, we ignore the fact that they likely wrote those chapters in a quiet office setting, not in the back of the school pickup lane. They aren't necessarily using their time to also shuffle kids from school to well-child check-ups and soccer practice.

The problem wasn't that I was getting this "simplifying my life" thing wrong over and over and over again. I was simply in a different season of life than the one I'd been in when I committed to a slower, simpler life—a far busier and more unpredictable one. What worked for me a couple of years ago wouldn't work today. Habits that work for time-management bros in an office setting fall apart when managing the unpredictability that comes with being the default parent. Our definition of simplicity must evolve with every new season we enter, role we assume, and challenge we face.

Just as minimalism often gives off a perfectionist aroma when it comes to home aesthetics and organization, simple living can do the same thing when it comes to time management. The same snake oil that guarantees that minimalism will safeguard us from untidiness tells us that simplicity will permanently protect us from ever feeling overly busy again. It says: if you're living intentionally enough, then you should never find yourself too busy to think straight. We've all read the pithy quotes and one-liners that try to solve our busyness with the broad brushstroke of simplicity.

But here's the thing I want to make clear. It's the linchpin of this entire book. Busy isn't the enemy. A full calendar isn't a failure.

It *can* be. Don't get me wrong. A crazy schedule can be the result of our inability to say no or our desire to keep up with the Joneses. It can be a result of not paying enough attention to where you're allocating your time and energy until you've gone on to schedule way, *waaaay* too much. Simplicity will certainly lighten your load. Throughout this book, I'll even offer you plenty of load-lightening, practical strategies.

But instead of suggesting that simplicity is the secret to permanently dodging all chaos, I want to offer it up as just another tool to help you navigate busy seasons with confidence. The trouble isn't with a busy schedule but rather with the hurried pace to which we've grown accustomed. At first glance, *busy* and *hurried* may appear to be synonyms, but at their core, they are very different. Busy is a matter of the calendar. Hurry is a matter of the heart.

Busyness can come from a full life, investing in what matters, and doing the next right thing. Sometimes it's just the result of being a living, breathing human person in charge of caring for other living, breathing human persons. No matter how I hack it, simplify it, slice it, dice it, and delegate it, I still, on occasion, find myself in over my head. Some days I even wonder why I'm paying property taxes when it seems I've taken up full-time residence in my car as a child chauffeur (#therealvanlife).

Society has made productivity one of the basic food groups, which has led us to this default setting of "too much"—too much stuff, too much to carry, and too much to do. It then tries to solve a too-much problem with *more*. The same way it tells us we need more bins to store the excessive amount of stuff in our homes, it also tells us we need more time-management strategies to multiply our minutes. We have, in turn, gotten both the problem and the solution all wrong. The trick is not learning to out-maneuver busyness or perfectly manage our time; it's learning how to be busy well.

While it was minimalism that set in motion my transformation in time management, it might be something entirely different for you. It could be something as drastic as a new diagnosis or loss of a job. Or perhaps it's as seemingly insignificant as a grocery store bathroom incident similar to my own. Maybe your kids are just entering elementary school and life is getting more hectic. Perhaps you're looking ahead at an almost empty nest, wondering where all the time went and what's next. Or maybe, like me, you're right in the messy middle, where your kids' hobbies are shifting from extracurricular to passions and you're left managing a family calendar that feels more like the trading floor of the New York Stock Exchange.

Whatever the reason, if you're taking a deeper look at how you're spending your days, keep looking. It can be an arduous task, but the reward is greater satisfaction with how you're using the only resource that truly matters in the end: time. And that is a worthy endeavor. Caring for our time, in my experience, takes relentless grace and a whole lot of pivoting. If your schedule feels like chaos right now, it's not a foregone conclusion that you're failing to curate the intentional life you long for. It may just be that you're in a busy season.

Remember that busy isn't always the villain we've made it out to be. Rather than seeing busy as the enemy, what if we could learn how to be busy well?

CHAPTER TWO

Seasonal Living

I took a long, hot shower this morning. Now, I usually do shower every day, and most of those showers are under scalding hot water. So what makes this shower notable enough to write about?

It's July, which means we're spending lots of time at our cottage. We've owned this cottage since our kiddos were babies. Jameson was three, Raegan was one, and Amelia wasn't even on our radar yet. She was simply a possibility.

Spending time by a body of water with little ones is two parts fun and twelve hundred parts stressful. You want everyone to have a good time, but it only takes one wrong move for things to go terribly wrong. I spent most of our time at the cottage during the last decade in a constant state of hypervigilance.

To ensure the safety of our children, I installed a series of obstacles so secure it would have required a *Mission Impossible*–style breach for anyone shorter than four feet tall to reach the water. First, there was a fence bordering the entire water line with a gate leading to the dock. I had a spring-close hinge installed on that gate door so that nobody could accidentally leave it open. The latch and lock were intentionally affixed to the *water* side of the gate. This way it could only be opened by those tall enough to reach over the top.

As if that weren't enough, I put latches and baby gates everywhere. It was next to impossible for small children to even reach the grass, let alone the fence that led to the water. There was a baby gate on the deck, a burglar bar affixed to the sliding door, and childproof doorknob covers on the front door and inside of every child's bedroom. Oh, and we put another baby gate at the bottom of the staircase and always moved a sofa table in front of the back door before going to bed for the night. Just in case.

If ever I dared to take a short afternoon nap, it was always on the living room couch, directly next to the double-locked slider door leading to the lakeside of the home. I was basically a bridge troll, half asleep, always on alert: "None shall pass."

Showering, however, was something I couldn't get around. It felt like the crack in my armor. An opportunity for error. If I was going to take a shower, it had to be fast. Even if the kids were sleeping or safely secured in front of a movie, I'd shower as fast as humanly possible, keeping the bathroom door slightly ajar so I could randomly shout out to make sure they were still inside. They always were.

Today, though, I stood lazily in the shower. Baby gates are a thing of the past, the fence has long since been removed, and my teenage son was fishing off the dock—by himself. We can now leave our kids home alone while we go for a morning jog or evening dinner date. Back in our baby gate phase, this season of life seemed lightyears away. We've come so far.

Don't get me wrong: I'm still a crazy person about water safety. But the level of vigilance I once had to maintain at all hours of the day and night is no longer necessary. And it's a beautiful gift.

SEASONAL LIVING

Of all the factors you face, the particular season of life you're in has the single biggest impact on the fullness of your calendar. Yet it's also the most commonly overlooked variable when people talk and write about time management. It's easy to oversimplify life's seasons, dividing them into childhood, adulthood, maybe parenthood, and, hopefully, the golden years. When it comes to time management, however, we have got to get much more specific.

There are seasons of significant progress and seasons of paralytic waiting, seasons of painful growth and seasons of joyful celebration. There are seasons of grief and seasons of euphoria, seasons of being a child and perhaps seasons of caring for one, seasons of rigid schedules and seasons of spontaneous adventures. You somehow managed to live through the season of being a teenager, but now maybe you're wondering if you can possibly survive *raising* one. There are seasons that are fast-paced and overwhelming, and seasons that move at a slower, steadier, and more manageable pace.

It's possible that you don't even realize which season you're in until you're looking back on it in the rearview mirror. Learning to identify if you're in a busy season is a critical first step.

A busy season is simply a period when your calendar is fuller than usual—when, despite your desire for a slightly slower pace, you've got many places to be and things to do. If you find that you're spending more time in your car than on your couch, you might be in a busy season. If you're secretly hoping a thunderstorm will roll in and cancel baseball tonight, you might be in a busy season. When you ambitiously order groceries for your weekly meal plan but find the only thing you have time for is another stop at Jimmy John's, you might be in a busy season. If you just can't seem to find the time or energy for the activities that fill you up, you might be in yet another busy season.

THE SIMPLICITY FALLACY

Have you ever noticed what's missing from home decor magazines, renovation show reveals, and ads for closet organization systems?

Reality.

They always put their best face forward with picture-perfect design trends that would make even the most minimalist monk swoon. What they don't show you is the everyday stuff: the muddy rain boots, the school picture forms, the lunch boxes haphazardly tossed on the dining table, and the guinea pig hay wildly kicked out on the floor. They don't highlight the syrup ring left on the counter, the basketball markings scuffed on the kitchen door jamb, or the inside-out leggings on the bathroom floor with the underwear still inside them.

When it comes to simple living and time management, it's often displayed by gurus, creators, and advertisers via the same dog-and-pony show. As a messy procrastinator with a tendency toward overbooking my life, I've devoured quite a few time-management books, articles, and podcasts over the years. I've always been on the hunt for ways to systemize my day, get more done, and still be a person in the process. What I typically end up with are practical time-management strategies that look good on the outside, maybe work well in an office setting, but tend to fall apart when the first kid tests positive for the flu.

Here you are, trying to time-block your day, habit-stack your goals, and meal-plan your heart out—and the next thing you know the whole week has gone to hell in a handbasket. Suddenly your whole day revolves around sanitizing doorknobs and knocking back shots of vitamin D oil with an elderberry gummy chaser. What time-management books can't account for, *this book included*, is the very season of life *you* are in at a given moment.

That's why I've grown to develop a bit of a love–hate relationship with the way the simple living movement has historically addressed the concept of time management. The term *time management* alone raises red flags for me. As a vocal advocate for simplifying every single facet of life, I've found it's easy to oversimplify what it means to live simply. We try to fast-track our way to a less overwhelming home and calendar, forgetting the variables that can't always be predicted. We're left wandering in and out of chaos, assuming we just aren't managing our time as we should.

Early on, as I was actively working to downshift my calendar and create more breathing room in my day—a vital component for living busy well—I stumbled across a heartwarming quote about simplifying our lives. I of course turned it into a pretty little digital image and shared it on social media.

I'm not going to share the specific quote with you because my goal isn't to throw the author under the bus. The line itself is great. The trouble is with our overgeneralization of its application.

Later that week, my cousin Amanda sent me a screenshot of it and asked, "Hey! Practically speaking, how would one go about doing this?"

I paused, honestly wondering what about it she didn't understand. *Just stop doing too many things. Cut back. Simplify your calendar the way you'd simplify a closet. What is there not to get?* My response was a little more diplomatic than that, but I felt the quote was relatively self-explanatory.

It's been years now since Amanda asked me how to practically apply that time-management philosophy. I had completely forgotten about that brief conversation until recently, when I found myself yet again doggy-paddling through my day, fighting to find enough time to get everything done. That's when it finally hit me.

You see, back when she was asking for a bit of practical advice, I was in an entirely different season of life than she was in. My preschool-aged kids had afternoon nap schedules and early bedtimes, while hers were in middle and high school. While it has now become countercultural to not put infants in club sports, I was at a stage of life when it was relatively easy to intentionally dodge unnecessary extracurricular activities. After all, my kids were too young to really care what we did with our time. As long as they had plenty of time to build living room forts, they were good. The only calendar I had to combat back then was my own.

Fast-forward to today, and what were once just community sports we could opt in or out of have become my kids' *passions*. Missing basketball practice means missing out on playing time. Not committing to attend *all* theater practices can mean not getting cast in the production at all. I'm no longer making the occasional playdate so *I* can spend time with a friend. We're now at the point where we're helping our kids cultivate meaningful friendships—some of which could span their lifetimes. How we spend our time is no longer solely up to Paul and me. My kids are old enough to get a say, and that has left us far busier than we thought we'd ever allow ourselves to become again.

YOU ARE HERE

When we are filling our calendars, making commitments, or setting personal goals, our current season of life should be the first thing we assess. Yet we miss it. Instead, we compare our morning routines, workout regimens, volunteer hours, and side hustles to others', ignoring our own reality. Pinpointing the season we're in is a fundamental first step in *real* time management. Without it, it's next to impossible to create a doable plan of action.

Not first acknowledging what season you're in would be like setting out on a five-mile hike without first finding the "You Are Here" marker on the trail map. You can't possibly know which way to go, how long it will take, or how to get home if you don't first orient yourself to your current location. You might set out on the wrong trail only to find yourself with another five miles to go as the sun sets and the park closes. The next thing you know, you're forced to use the survivalist strategies you learned watching *Alone*. (For the record, I do think I could build a stellar lean-to shelter if I had to. But I digress.)

Knowing and embracing the season you're in will allow you to set more realistic and reachable goals. The personal, professional, or family goals you set will be largely influenced by the season you're presently in. Reaching your goals shouldn't be a piece of cake, of course; they are goals for a reason. But when we take our real lives into account first, we'll set goals we stand a chance at reaching. A bit of context goes a long way and allows us to stop heading back to the drawing board every time reality interrupts our overly idealistic time-management plan.

I've come to learn that it isn't so much *time management* I loathe; it's the idea that time can or should be scripted, replicated, or universally systematized. You may be handed a syllabus during your first day of college classes, but nobody is doling them out outside of academics. We don't get to know every turn and obstacle coming at us down the pipeline.

Your life is going to look a heck of a lot different than mine, or your sister-in-law's, or the small business guru you follow on Instagram. While they may post the best inspirational quotes online, they could be in an entirely different season than you are right now. They're not working your job, dealing with your extended family, managing your family calendar, or walking in your footsteps. They may not have woken up at 3 a.m. to a puking child and had to cancel their entire day before it even started. In a self-help world, it's easy to miss the most obvious caveat: The way in which we manage our time is largely dependent on the season of life we're in.

What happens when a family with teenage kids tries to implement the same family calendar as a couple with young kids? It doesn't work. If your kids are grown and out of the house, your days will look far different than those of a young family navigating toddler naps and nursing newborns. And if you're kid-free, growing your career, or living that DINK life (double income, no kids), how you execute your mornings will look far different than parents getting three kids out the door to school before heading off to work. If you're a stay-at-home parent with a partner who has a job outside the home, your days will never mirror each other's.

My daughter and I both wear glasses, and both of us have a relatively mild prescription. But we can't use each other's glasses. I'm nearsighted and she's farsighted. If your efforts at time management feel more like a practice in wasting time than using it well, perhaps it's because you're looking at it through someone else's set of lenses.

Or take jeans: We don't all feel good wearing the same brand, size, color, and cut of jeans, right? While "one size fits all" can apply to things like earmuffs and gardening gloves, it just can't with jeans. And it can't with your time either. Trying to replicate someone else's "perfect morning routine" is just as uncomfortable as trying to fit into someone else's jeans. Both must be individualized to the life you live and the season in which you're living.

There is a time and place for participating in a triathlon, but I can assure you it's probably not going to be eight weeks after birthing a baby. Now perhaps that seems like an obvious one, but it's literally something I considered.

NO. YOU'RE NOT DOING THAT.

I sat at the nurse's station, talking with my coworkers about an upcoming local mini triathlon. I'd never participated in a triathlon before or run anything more than a 5K. But my naive, overly ambitious, nesting brain thought it sounded like a great idea. With roughly a month left of my first pregnancy, I figured, *What better way to get back in shape two months after giving birth than biking, swimming, and running multiple miles?*

Thankfully, my friend, who also happened to be my obstetrician, looked up at me from across the nurse's station as if she was talking to a lunatic and said, "No. You're not doing that."

Weeks later, with my first baby attached to me all hours of the day and night, I breathed a sigh of gratitude that someone had brought me back down to reality.

Seasonal living involves first getting your bearings, identifying exactly where you are, and *then* setting expectations. You wouldn't stomp through a foot of snow to your garden in the dead of winter expecting to harvest fresh green beans. Winter is not the time for green beans. But we expect ourselves to produce results as if we don't have small children to manage, boards to study for, or an entire book to write.

Seasonal living means recognizing that right now (not *never*) might not the best time to start a cookie-decorating business—or if it is, knowing that something else will have to give. Perhaps you need to hold off on adding dinner plans to your calendar for a couple months, pass on volunteering for the school Fund Run, or say "nope" when your kids ask to sell their crafts at the school makers market while you're trying to pack your home for a move. *Just speaking from experience.*

The fact is, there will be seasons when your calendar is fuller than others or when you won't have as much control over it as you'd like. When you know ahead of time that the positive habits you've adopted *will* get hijacked by a stomach virus, family crisis, infant sleep regression, or sudden change in employment, it's really quite freeing.

Let's pause here because I want to make sure there isn't any confusion. I'm *not* saying that trying to manage your time well during certain seasons is a lost cause. (Though there will certainly be weeks where it might be; take-out dinners and school hot lunches for the win.) I *am* saying that rather than trying to avoid, resist, or resent our busy seasons when they hit, we can lean into them. Instead of merely hacking through them like a dense jungle with a machete, hoping we happen upon a clearing, we can find the calm we're after by embracing the density in our current calendar.

Busy seasons are typically accompanied by a bit of chaos, frequent changes in plans, and the occasional sense of being absolutely overwhelmed. We don't have to continue to be blindsided but can instead anticipate them. We can grow to expect the unexpected, knowing we're always just one positive strep test away from household anarchy.

I know, I sound like a Debbie Downer. But I'm not suggesting that you simply lie down and succumb to the overwhelm. Instead, I want you to be better prepared for the wild turns as they come—to lean into them and to stay alert to changing conditions, so you can embrace the moments that matter right in the middle of that chaos. Picture it like escaping quicksand or a Chinese finger trap: the harder you fight it, the tighter it gets. The only way to make enough space to maneuver out of it is by relaxing and leaning into it.

We can win the war against busy by setting down our weapons and realizing we've been fighting the wrong enemy all along. It isn't our busyness we need to address; it's our hurried state of living.

TIP FOR BEING BUSY WELL: BREAK THE SCRIPT

In their book *The Power of Moments*, Chip and Dan Heath dive into the importance of crafting peak moments throughout life. These are memorable moments that stand out above others. The fascinating thing is that these peak moments don't have to be elaborate or expensive to qualify. One way to create more of them is to simply "break the script"—to defy expectations and step outside your typical routines. Script-breaking events can vary from a big adventure to a pleasant disruption in your normal evening routine. "By breaking the script," they say, "we can lay down a richer set of memories."

When you're in the thick of a busy season, the last thing you need is another disruption to your plans. Yet when we break the script on purpose, it can create sweet moments of connection and little high points that help sustain us. One way I like to break the script is to proclaim, "Popcorn for Dinner Night." Nothing bolsters connection around our house quite like giant bowls of buttery popcorn for dinner in front of a family movie. We don't have to simplify out of necessity. We can opt for a simpler route while making memorable moments in the process. Instead of more pizza or yet another grilled chicken dinner, popcorn for dinner can break the script in a fun and easy way.

CHAPTER THREE

The Unhurried Life

If you've ever been to the beach with young kids, you know it's a whole thing. Taking a solo parenting trip to the beach with toddlers could be used as a training exercise to help Navy Seals develop resilience and grit.

So when friends invited me to spend a kid-free day with them at Lake Michigan, I jumped at the opportunity. Having just visited with my kids a few weeks prior, I was eager for a little uninterrupted adult conversation and a whole lot of Audible. Lake Michigan becomes a partially frozen death trap in the winter, but in the dead of summer it can be a tropical paradise.

When we arrived, I laid out my beach towel and hightailed it to the shore to dip my hot, sandy feet in the cool lake water. What I felt quite literally took my breath away. It—was—freezing.

Not just an "Oh wow, that's colder than I remember" kind of freezing. No, it was more like a "medically not recommended to swim" kind of freezing. I'm talking painfully cold. I looked up and noticed that while the lake is normally peppered with swimmers, nobody else was in the water that day.

I was confused. Just a few of weeks ago I had visited with my kids, and it was relatively warm—warm enough for handstand contests and wading through the waves looking for beach glass. What happened?

Apparently, it's what's known as an Ekman spiral. Water molecules on the surface shift with a northern wind, and this, in turn, forces the water into a spiraling motion, bringing water from deep beneath the surface directly to the top. I imagine it's sort of how a ceiling fan circulates cooler air. You end up with a sudden plummet in water temperature as water molecules that haven't seen the light of day are now hanging out on top. One day you're swimming for hours, and then a few days later that same water is so cold it feels like it's trying to murder you. It turned out that water temps that weekend registered in the mid to low fifties.

I always assumed water temperatures only change due to *external* forces, like cooler summer nights or lots of rain. Sure, those factors will cause temps to fluctuate a bit; but it's changes *beneath* the surface that have the most drastic and noticeable impact.

INTERNAL EKMAN SPIRAL

I thought I was simply getting a tidier home. That's it. That's all I was really after when I started dabbling in minimalism. I had no idea what was waiting beneath the surface.

In one small but significant moment, I realized I wasn't just bad at keeping house; it was simply all the *keeping* that was the problem. I still had jeans dating back to high school piled in my closet. We had serving ware we'd received as a wedding gift—which we had never even used—stacked on shelves in the basement. I'd held on to every gift ever given me, and we had enough sippy cups in my cabinets to hydrate a small army of toddlers.

It was then I learned that I wasn't the kind of person who managed an overabundance of stuff well, and I no longer cared to spend my life trying. I came to realize the secret to keeping house is actually *keeping* as few things as possible.

What I thought was just a simple home transformation forced me to address areas I'd kept out of reach. Minimalism had a sort of Ekman spiral effect on me. It was a classic case of one thing leading to another. The next thing I knew, I was confronting things like comparison, fear, scarcity, and busyness. Reducing my wardrobe led me to stop shopping for new clothes, which then led me to reevaluate how I used my free time. If shopping was no longer an extracurricular activity, how exactly did I intend to use my newfound free time? I was surprised to discover just how interconnected my actions and habits were with my preconceived ideas about material possessions and consumerism.

My cabinets and closets were always disorganized and cluttered too, and I just figured it was due to our home's sparse closet space or the fact that I'm not all that great at interior design and home organization. In reality, though, it had little to do with any of those reasons and more to do with fear. My scarcity mentality led me to hold onto many "what if I need it someday" items. You know, just in case.

It's the same thing with our calendars as well. On the surface, feeling overwhelmed by your to-do list can appear to be just a simple issue of overcommitment. While that certainly may be a contributing factor, and one you need to address, I've found overcommitment to be more of a side effect than the root cause. The deeper enemy is our habit of hurried living.

THE DIFFERENCE BETWEEN HURRY AND BUSY

While *busy* is having a lot to do, *hurry* is doing those things while stressed, distracted, or rushed. Hurry looks like moving through your day, whether it's busy or not, with a frenetic stride. It's a way of life marked by feeling overwhelmed, chaotic, worried, distracted, and disconnected. Nothing sucks the joy out of your day more than feeling constantly overwhelmed by your calendar, mentally drained by decision fatigue, and too digitally distracted to be present for the moments that matter.

A number of factors can lead to hurry. Did you start your day with the news rather than solitude, prayer, or reflection? Have you been donating too much of your attention to social media? Did you overbook your week? Are you letting yourself spiral through all the "what ifs" instead of handling what's happening in front of you right now? Did you set unrealistic expectations for yourself or your loved ones? Are you avoiding issues by shopping, reorganizing, or planning an escape route disguised as a vacation?

Sure, sometimes you have to literally hurry, like when you're running to your car before it starts to downpour or hurrying to your gate to catch your connecting flight. Hurried living, though, isn't just about the number on the speedometer. Hurry is the reason we keep needing to step on the gas in the first place. It's a state of mind that negatively impacts *how* we use our limited time, energy, and attention. When you hear me reference *hurried living* or *hurry* throughout this book, I want you to think about the habits, actions, commitments, and preconceived ideas that leave us functioning in a state of overwhelm more often than not.

Busyness is an unavoidable reality from time to time, but hurry is something we can start to safeguard ourselves against.

The ironic thing about hurried living is that you don't even need to be busy or rushed to find yourself there. You don't need a jam-packed family calendar or extended work hours to feel hurry rise within you. There have been many times during slower seasons when I've felt overwhelmed by it. Here I am, with a normal-person number of things to do. And yet when my husband asks me if I can call a plumber, I want to hop in my car and drive until I run out of road. It makes no sense. What's up?

The likely culprit during those times is tapped attention. If I spend my leisurely Saturday scrolling through social media, running meaningless errands, or devoting my attention to unresolvable family drama, I find myself just as mentally exhausted as if I'd spent my day at work, managing a kindergarten norovirus outbreak—fewer bodily fluids, sure, but the same mental exhaustion. When we're devoting our attention and energy to the wrong sort of things or giving ourselves far too little time to recover, we're left feeling overstimulated and overwhelmed for no good reason whatsoever.

In her book *The Power of Fun*, Catherine Price refers to scrolling through social media as "fake fun." She explains it this way:

> For many of us, a lot of what we do "for fun" isn't fun at all. Instead, we spend much of our leisure time on "Fake Fun," a term I use to describe activities and possessions that are marketed to us as fun, that we work long hours to be able to afford, but that are ultimately meaningless or a waste of time—such as binge-watching shows to the point that our eyes glaze over, buying things we don't need, or mindlessly scrolling through social media for hours at a time. Fake Fun is numbing and leaves us empty when we're done. True Fun, on the other hand, makes us feel nourished and refreshed.

In the same way, hurried living leaves us with the illusion of productivity. We feel like we did a lot—yet when we take a closer look at where our time and attention went, it's hard to point to anything truly meaningful or productive.

Each of us responds to hurried living a little differently. Some of us might lock in and hustle harder, while others completely shut down. Instead of checking things off of our to-do lists, we procrastinate.

We put them off, hoping that our tasks, problems, or conflicts will somehow resolve themselves. When we're already overwhelmed, procrastinating can feel like the safer bet. Nine times out of ten, however, it only adds to our workload, leaving us more distracted and drained.

While being overly busy for too long is a one-way ticket to the hurried life, it isn't the only path there. Comparison, digital distraction, overthinking, conflict, shame, worry, procrastination, and misaligned priorities all reduce our capacity. We'll get to those later in the book. But the fact is that you don't need a busy schedule to live a hurried life. Once we address the deeper issues draining our capacity, we'll have far more time and attention left to devote to living well, even in the busier seasons of life.

Busyness gets a bad rap. I've heard it described as a "failure to prioritize" and as "a result of us doing too many things for too many people." Sure, those may leave you busy, but so might prioritizing well. And what if those "many people" are *your* people? Literal people you made who depend on you for the many things they need? The busyness they lead you into doesn't have to be viewed as a detriment to your well-being.

Purposeful work, carefully chosen with intention and care, can leave you tired as well. But the exhaustion you feel from that purposeful work is a particular *kind* of tired. Like muscle pain after a good long workout, it's meant to strengthen you. Just because something leaves you overwhelmed or running in a few directions at once doesn't mean you've failed to properly prioritize. When we stop looking down on our full calendars, it opens up a whole new world of possibilities for how to tackle them strategically.

Eliminating commitments isn't the only solution to feeling overwhelmed. Thank goodness, because reducing commitments isn't always an option. Not all commitments are created equally. In fact, during specific seasons of life, busyness is an essential component of the human existence. If Thomas Edison hadn't been busy making the lightbulb, where would we be? If J. K. Rowling hadn't been busy writing *Harry Potter* and persistent in her commitment to get it published, there would be no butterbeer. Busyness isn't the enemy. In fact, it can be a vital element to innovation.

If a business is slow for too long, a company won't stay in business for long. If a student isn't busy studying when final exams roll around, it's concerning. When our kids develop friendships and hobbies of their own, we may end up driving them places more than we're used to, but our resulting busyness is a sign they are growing up and becoming more independent.

Being more present and attentive to the things that matter doesn't have to come at the expense of our commitments, jobs, and extracurricular activities. We don't need to pare down our family calendar until there is nothing left. You can be busy and present, but you can't be present without being attentive.

In elementary school, we all memorized the three R's: reduce, reuse, and recycle. However, I don't recall anyone explaining the first two to me at all, only recycling. I remember coming home from school, appalled that our family hadn't been recycling and demanding answers. Yet while recycling can be important, it isn't the most effective method for long-term environmental sustainability. Instead, our focus should be on reducing the number of material possessions we own, buying secondhand, and repairing our things instead of replacing them.

Recycling is more appealing than reducing or reusing, though, because it doesn't force us to change our lifestyle. We can keep on overconsuming and buying fast fashion. If we recycle a few things along the way and donate our excess belongings before buying new ones, we feel justified in our not-reducing and not-reusing.

The same goes for the way we approach time management. We tend to focus on creating more time by time blocking our day, buying a better planner, sacrificing our own hobbies, or rising a little earlier, while ignoring the fact that we are in the habit of starting and ending our day plugged into screens. Here we are, complaining about our dwindling capacity—all while donating large amounts of our attention to worrying, micromanaging, or issues that aren't ours to carry. Or we plan elaborate and expensive vacations to connect with our family while spending the rest of our weeks overwhelmed and distracted.

Cultivating an unhurried life starts by looking beyond the obvious offenders, the ones on the surface, and looking deeper to where we've been devoting our attention.

MANAGING THE UNPREDICTABLE

While many things that cause us to live in a hurried state of mind are self-induced, sometimes extenuating circumstances outside our control are to blame. Things like car trouble, last-minute game time changes, illness, injury, cancelled flights, and weather all can come out of nowhere.

The overly simplistic "simple living" philosophy can leave us feeling as though we should be able to control all the variables that tend to leave us overwhelmed. If we just "eliminate the things that don't matter," then we'll get a better grip on the things that do. That *is* an effective strategy—to a point. But in my nearly ten years of actively and effectively simplifying my life, I've found that it just isn't always an option. We can't always eliminate our way into an unbusy life.

There are five people in my home, each with things that matter to them and a multitude of extenuating circumstances confiscating our free time and mental energy. Things like forgotten homework assignments. Work crises that arise at 4:50 p.m. Asthma flare-ups. Cascading illnesses stringing us along. Simple clerical errors that leave us rushing to the dentist appointment we thought was tomorrow.

Just two days ago, while in the midst of this very busy season, I sliced through a loaf of bread without properly situating my fingers first and quite literally chopped the very tip of my finger clean off. Not through the bone or anything, but enough of it that I was able to find a sliver of flesh on the counter. (You can't make this stuff up.)

You want to know what I don't have time for right now? A useless finger slowing down my typing of this book and making it nearly impossible to do my daughter's hair for opening night of her theater production—which is tonight.

It happens all the time, though. There you are, holding it all together, and out of nowhere, you're shoulder-checked by a crisis you couldn't possibly have accounted for. So what's the solution? Are we doomed to live in a state of hurry? Are we destined to ping-pong back and forth between having it all together and falling apart? Because sometimes I've wondered.

Well, I have good news and bad news. The good news is that no, you do not have to live in that frenetic state for all your days. The bad news is that you are guaranteed to experience it from time to time.

Apart from living by yourself on a private island off the coast of Norway, there really isn't anything you can or should do to prevent every busy season. When you're living a full life, it's bound to bubble over on occasion. If you've happened to discover a method for avoiding chaos for the entirety of a lifetime, I'd love to read your book on the subject. But I'm willing to bet it's still just an insurance plan with a term limit.

There is no perfect equation to dodging every single season of busyness. Instead, it's a matter of creating a life with enough breathing room and grace to readily absorb the chaos that accompanies those busier seasons of life. Those moments of chaos or seasons of busyness don't have to be a way of life or send us spiraling into hurry. You can take on a posture of flexibility and agility so you can pivot when the time comes. Because it will.

We wind up making our busier seasons harder than they need to be by overcommitting our time or relinquishing our mental energy to trivial matters. A couple of chapters from now, we will talk more about what to do when unexpected circumstances hijack our capacity. But first, we need to be sure we're spending our time, energy, and attention in the correct quadrant.

THE EISENHOWER MATRIX

Created by Dwight Eisenhower and made popular by Steven Covey, the urgent versus important matrix is an excellent tool to help us better understand the differences between being busy and living hurriedly. Its principles can help us better allocate our limited capacity by categorizing our activities based on their urgency and importance or lack thereof.

Quadrant I includes tasks that are both urgent and important. These are time sensitive, pressing matters that require our immediate attention.

Quadrant II includes tasks that help prevent crises from occurring in the first place. Here we put activities such as exercise, organization, regular date nights, long-term planning, family time, and personal growth.

Activities in Quadrant III, while urgent, aren't all that important. These involve tasks such as responding to certain messages or phone calls, tasks we continue to perform out of obligation, or micromanaging issues that aren't really our responsibility.

Lastly, Quadrant IV includes tasks that are neither urgent nor important. These are tasks we add to our to-do lists out of habit, to distract ourselves, or to keep up with arbitrary productivity goals. In this quadrant we use our time to impulse shop, redecorate our homes, or scroll through social media.

While there are countless examples online, I've created my own, more personally relevant matrix, shown here, with some of the activities and responsibilities unique to me in this season.

When creating my own time-management matrix, I had the hardest time listing things that could fall into the *not important* categories. For the most part, I can easily identify which things are urgent and which aren't. Maybe it's all those years working as an OB triage nurse. I've got years of experience distinguishing between the pressing matters and the ones that can wait. However, I still found it surprisingly difficult to identify which things are *not important* at all. My brain likes to default to *everything* being important in one way or another.

Yet if everything is important, then *nothing* is. We'd never say out loud that folding laundry or replying to a family text thread is as important as, say, resolving an asthma attack, would we? Yet the way in which we expend our limited energy and allocate our attention may imply otherwise. We let ourselves get pushed and pulled by the *unimportant*, which in turn leaves us with very little time and

	Urgent	Not Urgent

Important	**Quadrant I**
	Urgent and Important
	
	Sick kids
	Book deadline
	Jameson's concussion
	   appointments
	Show week for my
	   daughter's theater
	   production
	Packing our home to move
		Quadrant II
		Not Urgent but Important
		
		Exercising
		Healthy meal planning
		Home improvement
		   decisions
		Quality family time
		Making appointments
		Coffee with friends
		Spending time outdoors
		Writing new articles for
		   my blog
		Cleaning and tidying
		Washing dirty clothes

Not Important	**Quadrant III**
	Urgent but Not Important
	
	Responding to certain
	   emails and text
	   messages
	Creating mountains out
	   of mole hills
	Making homemade
	   peanut butter (see
	   chapter 6)
	Any time-sensitive tasks
	   I perform out of
	   obligation
		Quadrant IV
		Not Urgent and
		Not Important
		
		Folding clean laundry
		Scrolling on social media
		Watching television
		Shopping for inessential
		   items
		Redecorating the house

energy to handle the truly important and urgent matters as they arise. When faced with those truly urgent and important matters, we're running on fumes, with nothing left in the tank to take them on. Instead of facing them with confidence, we cower in the corner, hoping this crisis will find a way to resolve itself. Being busy well starts by ensuring we're devoting the firstfruits of our capacity, so to speak, to the most important things in our lives. This will ensure we're fortifying our lives in a way that leaves us more prepared for, and better able to withstand, the unexpected.

When creating a solid budget, you wouldn't let entertainment and travel take their cut before paying for your housing, heat, and food, would you? We need to allocate our capacity in the same way: by ensuring the most important areas get what they need first before doling out what remains.

The more areas we misclassify as important and urgent, the easier it is to slip into hurried living. Can you think of any tasks you've made a top priority that, in fact, were just busywork? For me, it's feeling the need to run errands and respond to text messages immediately. But they're usually just nonurgent tasks disguised as urgent ones. Some days I've had plenty of time to effectively address tasks in Quadrant II but squandered it away by hopping between Quadrants III and IV. I pick up my phone to respond to a message—and the next thing I know, I'm looking for home renovation ideas on Pinterest. Or I start tidying my kitchen—and get lured into scrolling for new recipes.

Instead of spending our time away from work investing in soul-filling activities, planning for the busy week ahead, spending time outdoors, or having face-to-face coffee with a friend, we dive head-first into the unimportant activities of Quadrants III and IV. It's no wonder we're left feeling like we have no time.

According to time-management expert Stephen Covey, Quadrant II is the sweet spot. He says, "Effective people stay out of Quadrants III and IV, because urgent or not, they aren't important. They also shrink Quadrant I down to size by spending more time in Quadrant II."

For those prone to procrastination, putting off tasks can seem like an energy saver on the front end. But ultimately, it winds up costing us. The next thing you know, the simple question, "What's for dinner?" leaves you feeling like you've just been asked to pilot a transatlantic flight or perform brain surgery.

Why? Because when you put tasks off long enough, it forces them to migrate from Quadrant II into Quadrant I. The tasks you once had plenty of time to address become urgent. Suddenly the laundry you didn't stay on top of becomes an emergency because none of you have any clean clothes. It's pure hurried living at its finest. You're now forced to spend your time putting out fires in Quadrant I because you'd taken up full-time residence in the wrong quadrants. It feels as though you're always playing catch up with the most important tasks while wasting time on the insignificant ones.

When we live like this long enough, we become so well acclimated to the frenetic pace that anything else feels uncomfortable. I'm a fast talker. Because of that, when I listen to audiobooks, I always increase the speed. Sometimes books are narrated so slowly it's hard for me to pay attention—not because there's a right or wrong narration pace but because it's what I'm used to.

To be busy well, we must be willing to venture into uncharted waters, looking beyond what merely lies on the pages of our calendars. Things like overcommitment, unrealistic expectations, failing to prune, and the overconsumption of both material possessions and digital content pull at our limited capacity. The following chapters are geared toward helping you do just that. We're going to start slowing down, creating margin, quitting what isn't working, and confidently declining commitments we don't have the capacity for.

Slowing down and becoming more intentional with our time can feel unbearably difficult when we're accustomed to the chaotic pace of hurry. It's like how my broken closet doors and missing fingertip feel like just another day at the office. We're so used to our hurried way of life that slowing down feels like too uncomfortable of a change to make. Let me assure you that while facing what lies beneath the surface can be hard, in time the discomfort will ease. And you'll wonder what took you so long to make the change.

TIP FOR BEING BUSY WELL:
MAKE YOUR MATRIX

I want to encourage you to grab a sheet of paper or go ahead and write in this book to create your own matrix of urgent and important things (see p. 181 for a template for your matrix). Don't get stuck trying to make it perfect.

In my experience, the *important but not urgent* quadrant is the one to spend the most time on. This is where we highlight those things that matter most to us. And when we focus our time, energy, and attention on those activities, they pay dividends in the future.

CHAPTER FOUR

Be Mindful

The Art of Making and Keeping Margin

The older I've gotten, the more claustrophobic I've become. It's always been a bit of an issue since the fateful day when my friends left me in a locker. I had willingly gotten in, to see if I could fit, and then they left me there. Someone let me out only minutes later, but it felt like an eternity.

Now, the thought of being confined in close quarters—say, getting strapped into a rollercoaster—gives me the heebie-jeebies. When I do get suckered onto a rollercoaster by my thrill-seeking children, I go above and beyond to keep a good amount of margin between my body and the safety bar.

The last time I rode a roller coaster was at Universal Studios in Harry Potter World. Per my usual, I scooted forward a few subtle inches, took in a big breath, and lifted my heels off the ground to make myself as large as possible. Typically the attendant just whisks by, mindlessly pushing down and then pulling up on the safety bar to ensure it has been secured in place. This time, however, the attendant noticed what I was up to. Perhaps I wasn't as subtle as I thought. He tried pushing the bar down on me a little tighter as I leaned forward, fighting against him.

"Please," I said. "This is good enough. I promise I won't fall out . . .
please." He looked at me like I was a weirdo (because let's be honest,
I was acting like one). "Give me one more click," he negotiated. I
reluctantly complied, because—well, what else was I going to do? It
was snug, but there was just enough space for me and my insanity.
Yes, I'd rather risk flying off a rollercoaster somewhere over Florida
than spend ninety seconds locked between the seat and safety bar.

In this chapter, we are going to talk about why we need margin, how to create said margin, and when to push back when the
world tries to take it. Don't forget: it's imperative you view this time-
management principle through the lens of the season you are in at
this moment. Some seasons allow for more margin than others. That's
not a bad thing. It's just the truth. But margin can be made in every
season if we're willing to be flexible with its definition.

So what exactly do I mean by "margin"? As Richard Swenson so
beautifully puts it in his book, *Margin*, "Margin is the space between
our load and our limit. It is the amount allowed beyond that which is
needed." Margin is simply the space between activities. It's the time
we allot to take a breather, recover, get our bearings, get grounded,
be a person, or prepare for what's next.

Take the pages of this book, for example. If the words filled
every space from top to bottom and side to side—if there were no
margins—it would be hard to read. Eventually it might start to bother
our eyes and frustrate our focus. We'd be more prone to losing our
place or setting the book down altogether. The margins in a book
reduce our chances of becoming distracted and highlight the areas
we are meant to focus on.

This is what time margin does as well. It prevents us from becoming overwhelmed and distracted. It gives us a chance to live in the
moment rather than just get through it and then on to the next one.

When I refer to margin, I'm not talking about a vacation or sabbatical. Those are great, but they are not reliable sources of energy. Margin is simply the time we keep free during our regularly scheduled

lives. The assumption that margin must be a two-week international vacation or a full three-day weekend dedicated to doing nothing actually keeps us from prioritizing it at all. Because when you're in the thick of it, commitment-free time like that may be out of the question. *I'm looking at you, soccer season.*

Look at it this way: if margin is the space bordering the words in a book, then a vacation or sabbatical would be a completely empty journal. Both margin *and* extended time off are valuable, but they aren't the same thing. The occasional extended period of time dedicated solely to rest, leisure, or travel isn't enough to keep us from falling apart throughout the rest of the year. We need small amounts of margin in our regularly scheduled lives in order to keep hurry at bay.

Margin might look like the first Saturday after soccer season comes to an end—and as of right now, you don't have anywhere to be that day. It could be an evening after work when you don't have plans. Or maybe it's that one evening of the week during a busy season when the stars align, everyone is home, and you get to have dinner together as a family. And sometimes margin is just that awkward window between practice drop-off and pick-up—you know, when it's not worth driving all the way home but feels like too much time to just sit in your car. Those small, seemingly insignificant slivers of margin can be effective capacity fillers but only when we notice them, use them wisely, and push back against the pressure to fill them. If you find yourself chronically overwhelmed, perhaps it's because you've gotten in the habit of relinquishing your valuable margin to mindless scrolling or the relentless call to pack in more.

The amount of margin in our weeks will vary. During slower seasons we'll have more of it, and the margin we make can be easily maintained. Family dinners are a regular occurrence, and we feel rested and recharged. During chaotic seasons, however, margin can be hard to come by. If we do manage to find a sliver of free time, the chaos constantly threatens to envelop it. Here, it's hard to tell which way is up, and we're forced to spend much of our already small margin fighting off time invaders like we're intergalactic superheroes.

Let's put it in terms of beach flags, shall we? Our calendars ebb and flow much like changing water conditions at the beach. Some days the waters are calm. When this is the case, lifeguards fly a green flag telling beachgoers it's safe to swim. As the waves pick up, however, flags may progress from green to yellow to red and eventually to double red, progressively warning that swimming isn't safe.

We can look at our calendars the same way; we move from green to yellow, orange, and red depending on our fluctuating calendar conditions.

Your calendar is waving a green flag when life includes very few commitments outside your working hours. There is plenty of margin on your calendar, and you didn't even have to fight for it. Here you can easily devote time to loved ones and the activities that fill you up. You may even be on vacation, sabbatical, or enjoying an entire season free of extracurricular commitments.

It becomes a yellow flag when you have a rising but still manageable number of tasks, plans, and commitments to keep. Here, your calendar still boasts plenty of margin for rest, family time, healthy habits, and relationship-building in between those commitments. As my friend Nikki puts it, "Life is full, but not too busy." In my experience, this is the sweet spot.

Your calendar moves to orange when life really starts picking up. Here commitments collide and your margin begins to evaporate. It's still there, but now you must fight to maintain it and get creative with its definition. This may look like a sports-heavy season, the end of the school year, the holidays, or a notoriously busy time of year at work. Perhaps it's summertime and you've got multiple kids to cart to different camps. Or maybe your car hit a recliner on the highway after it fell out of some dude's truck, and now your family is down a vehicle for the foreseeable future. *(Just me?)* Whatever the reason, if you're a human person, you *will* find yourself in this more chaotic season from time to time. The key is to make sure you're never here for very long lest you run the risk of moving into the red zone.

Red is the danger zone. This is a pace we want to avoid at all costs. It's when your margin has been reduced to nothing and you're running from one thing to another like life is a relay race. Except instead of passing the baton off to someone else, it's just you, running one leg after another after another.

How to Be Busy is about developing strategies to help us pivot from season to season and avoid the dreaded margin deprivation. I don't want to give the impression that your whole life can be lived in the green zone if you just simplify enough; remember, that's the book I *didn't* write. I'm hoping to move us away from that very flawed narrative. But we *can* use simplicity and intentionality to navigate life's chaotic turns with flexibility and grace. While the orange season is inevitable, my hope is that the principles you find here will help you spend a little more time in the green and yellow zones and as little as possible in the red.

MARGIN DEPRIVATION

This concept likely needs no introduction. The words *margin deprivation* say it all, don't they? It's when we're completely deprived of the margin we desperately need. I'm sure you've felt the effects of margin deprivation at one point in time or another. I know I have. This is the land of the hurried, when family dinners are only a mirage and it feels like your never-ending to-do list is trying to strangle you. Here we see our loved ones only in passing, struggle with decision fatigue, and feel overwhelmed practically all the time. It's just too much.

When we're margin deprived, we may have a shorter fuse or find ourselves absolutely undone by the most insignificant hiccups. We have no time to tidy as we go, so the messes pile up. Being present and engaged? Those aren't even on the table, because we've got to stay focused on our next move. There's no time to slow our stride, even for a second, because if we do, we'll surely lose our balance on the very delicate tightrope that is the margin-deprived life. Here, we're even more prone to sickness and injury as well. *Exhibit A: The missing tip of my finger.*

On top of that, we start missing emails, forgetting appointments, and dropping the ball. God forbid someone try to toss us another, because we'll surely drop them all. Here it feels as though we're always teetering on the verge of a breakdown.

One wrong move, missed exit, or fevered child will surely bring this delicate house of cards to the ground. Frankly, I'm just not the best version of myself when I don't have enough time to even catch my breath, let alone my sanity.

Over the course of the next few chapters, we are going to address exactly *how* to go about making more margin in our days so we can steer far and wide of margin deprivation. We'll dive into the practice of under-committing, learn to say no, work to reduce our screen time, offload inessential tasks, and delegate where we can. For the remainder of this chapter, however, we're going to discuss how best to utilize the margin we do manage to make.

HOW WE USE OUR MARGIN MATTERS

How you use your margin matters as much, if not more, than how much margin you have during a given season. Margin can only be beneficial if it isn't wasted, donated, or hijacked. If used wisely, it can offer a potent shot of presence and joy. We've got to be intentional with our margin, because if we aren't paying close attention, the next thing we know, it's gone.

As a firm believer in the one-size-does-*not*-fit-all approach to things like motherhood, minimalism, and time management, I hesitate to tell you exactly *how* to use your margin. So let's start with what *not* to do. For example, don't waste your margin responding to needless text messages, replying to phone calls, mindlessly scrolling social media, or squeezing in more plans.

Here are a few ways of wasting my margin that I typically regret:

- Consuming social media
- Texting
- Worrying
- Running nonurgent errands or impulse shopping

Instead, use your margin to do something that might offer some reprieve for your brain down the road. The "Lazy Genius," Kendra Adachi, calls it the Magic Question. Ask yourself, "What can I do now to make life easier later?"

Keep in mind that the answer may or may not be geared toward productivity. Sometimes the thing that future you needs most is a nap, a moment of connection, or a bit of *true* fun.

Here are ways I personally like to use my margin:

- Playing a game of Uno or Checkers with my kids
- Exercising
- Mushroom hunting
- Drinking tea and reading a novel
- Tending to my pumpkin patch
- Brain dumping the things weighing me down
- Prepping dinner ahead of time
- Fishing off the dock
- Taking a walk outdoors
- Taking an eight-minute power nap
- Rebounding the basketball for my son

For the purpose of this book, I've categorized the use of margin into three categories: (1) personal time, (2) relationship building, and (3) productivity. Let's take a deeper look at each of these and the impact they have.

PERSONAL TIME

You can use margin for personal time in a variety of ways. It may offer you a chance to participate in a book club, spend time outdoors, read a book, take a nap, learn to make sourdough bread, or tap maple trees.

If you've got young ones at home, your personal time may be practically nonexistent. When mine were little, the only free time I could find some days was lying on the couch and hiding under a blanket. How they didn't know I was there is beyond me. I could spy on them through the small holes in my afghan blanket, but they couldn't see me. It was a delightful few minutes where nobody could demand something of me. Now I can write this in the quiet, at 6:00 a.m. on a Saturday when my teenagers are still fast asleep. I'm living proof that your season will change.

I know. I know. I sound like an old lady telling you, "It goes by so fast!" It doesn't go by fast, though. It just goes by. Hang in there, young parents; more personal time is on the horizon. It can feel like an eternity when you're in the middle of it, but I assure you, you'll get your personal time back again sooner than you think.

RELATIONSHIP BUILDING

One of the biggest benefits of margin is the time it provides to deepen your relationships with the people you love. It frees you up to enjoy coffee with friends, date nights with your partner, and quality time with your kids. I wouldn't sprint around my driveway in 48-degree weather to rebound a basketball for just anyone. Yet when our evenings are chaos-free, that's often where you'll find me:

chasing down shots, tossing the ball back to my teenage son, and talking trash—*obviously*.

Making and maintaining margin gives us time to both deepen our current relationships and make new ones. With breathing room in our schedules, we'll find we have the capacity to linger in the lobby after church to chat or strike up a conversation with a teammate's family after a basketball game. When I'm operating in the red, I keep my head down and immediately head for the door. "Ain't nobody got time for that" becomes my mantra. But with margin in our day, we have time to invest in the very community we will need to lean on during the more chaotic seasons.

PRODUCTIVITY

In a perfect world, we'd be free to devote all our margin to only the most soul-filling of activities. We'd get a massage, grab coffee with a friend, take a cozy nap, bake cookies with our kids, go for a run, knit a hat, read a book, or forage for mushrooms. But sometimes, desperate times call for desperate measures. If you're teetering into that red zone, running on little to no margin at all, using your last remaining sliver of free time to check a few things off your to-do list might be the greatest gift you can give your future self that day. Printing the pictures for your child's school project, dropping off the donation pile in the back of your car, making that appointment you've been putting off, or finally folding the wrinkly laundry: such things can give you more margin in the future.

For those who easily succumb to hustle culture, you might be in the habit of using *all* your margin for productivity. Yes, using your margin to check things off your to-do list can be a valuable strategy for freeing up time in the future for more meaningful moments of margin. But beware this strategy: while those activities may leave you feeling a bit of relief, they won't necessarily leave you recharged. What starts out as providing relief can quickly evolve into the chronic habit of turning all your margin into another opportunity for productivity.

Be careful how much margin you allocate here because while productivity can be a time saver, it's not a capacity filler.

PUT FIRST THINGS FIRST

The secret to using our margin for filling back up is to prioritize tasks before they become urgent. Think back to the time matrix we talked about in the previous chapter. When we steer clear of the time-wasting quadrants and prioritize tasks in Quadrant II, we reduce how much time we're forced to spend putting out fires in Quadrant I. This, in turn, leaves us with more control over our down time.

Now, you may be thinking, "Thanks a lot, Rachelle. I'm drowning over here—and you're suggesting I go back in time to focus on areas before they become an emergency?" I'm well aware that time travel isn't really a realistic time-management strategy. Understanding and utilizing the time-management matrix may not get you out of the mess you're in right now, but it can help you avoid landing here again in the future.

Remember, the hurried life isn't only found within the orange or red seasons of life. If you aren't careful, you can live hurriedly no matter what your calendar looks like. It's quite possible to spend your time within a green zone on hurried life activities. You can take your family vacation and drain your mental energy by using it to create reels for Instagram instead of pursuing the *real* connection you're after. You could take your day off and squander it on online shopping, overthinking, or getting caught in a drama-filled text thread.

On the bright side, we can also find margin during those busier seasons as well. A brief, silent walk around the block can work wonders for your soul in a pinch. It's not how much time you have but what you do with that time that will make or break you.

TIP FOR BEING BUSY WELL:
FIND THE AIR POCKET

In 2013, a man named Harrison Okene was found alive, 100 feet below the sea. During a storm, a wave had overturned the ship he worked on, killing everyone else on board except him. He thankfully had managed to find safe haven in the bathroom prior to that wave hitting and found himself secured within a small air pocket within the ship. It was no small miracle when, *three days later*, divers found Okene alive during recovery efforts.

This story comes to mind every time I find myself drowning on dry ground. When I'm overwhelmed by a busy season or struggling to carve out time to recover, I think to myself, *Find the air pocket.* It's there; you just have to find it and refuse to fill it. If you only have a small pocket of margin right now, use it to take the deep breath, power nap, or soul-filling stroll your body needs.

CHAPTER FIVE

Be Bored

The Practice of Under-Committing

One Saturday in the dead of winter, I spent hours simmering a pot of homemade chicken broth on the stove. Our entire home smelled divine. After straining this pot of liquid gold into a large bowl in my sink, I momentarily turned away to cut veggies for soup.

Big mistake. My kids, who had been painting in the other room, had coincidently chosen that exact moment to come into the kitchen to wash the red paint off their tiny hands—directly over my giant bowl of broth. They were completely oblivious to what I was doing. To them, my broth just looked like a bowl of dirty water.

Upon returning to my broth, I found it now tinted red and covered with soapy bubbles. It took me a moment to process what had occurred, before loudly shouting, "*Nooo!*"

Everyone came running to the kitchen and then slowly cowered away as they realized one by one what they'd done. Paul frantically tried to remedy the situation, to no avail. Turns out you can't strain paint and soap out of broth. The damage was done. There was no saving my soap soup.

I silently slid into my slippers, turned away from the kitchen, walked out the front door, and just started walking. It was the dead of winter, but I didn't even need a coat for warmth. The rage was enough to heat me from the inside out. The only thing I truly needed in that moment was a large amount of space between myself and the guilty parties.

After a coatless lap or two around the block in my slippers, I texted Paul.

"Pizza?"

"Yup," he replied.

I had done everything right. I had diligently planned ahead, saving vegetable scraps and a couple chicken carcasses in preparation for my soup. I even got to work bright and early that day so the broth would have plenty of time to simmer on the stove. In a matter of seconds, however, all my effort and planning evaporated. It was all for nothing. Dinner was hijacked.

While this story pretty much sums up parenting in a nutshell, it's also representative of what often happens to even our best-laid plans. Unforeseen circumstances alter the course of our day all the time; yet when it happens, we're caught off guard. It could be something as simple as our newly cleaned kitchen floors being sabotaged by a bowl of spilled cereal.

Or maybe it's bigger.

CONCUSSION PROTOCOL

We were just a couple of weeks into an already full fall calendar when my son received a concussion in gym class. What I assumed would be a handful of days when he was down for the count turned into three months of doctor's appointments and therapies to help resolve lingering symptoms. That concussion took our tight but perfectly calibrated fall schedule and decimated it.

Because of that, I'm currently living through what just may be the busiest week I've ever experienced. My son had six doctor's appointments in four days and basketball practice every evening. (Don't worry; his basketball practice has been *extremely* modified to accommodate his injury. He already missed his entire soccer season and is desperately hoping to get the "all clear" before basketball concludes as well.)

And all this is occurring during show week for my daughter's theater group. Oh, and did I mention I'm on a book deadline? I'm currently hopping between writing these words, coordinating rides, and figuring out *how*, exactly, we'll pull this week off.

The thing is, we *had* plenty of margin, right before this now double red season. As it just so happened, we were sucker punched by unforeseen circumstances. Literally. One accidental blow to the head undid it all.

Perhaps your capacity has been obliterated by a job loss, crisis at work, or newly appointed promotion. Maybe it's something as insignificant as a growth spurt that leaves you scrambling to find your daughter dress shoes for her choir concert tonight, or something as overwhelming as a close friend or family member filing for divorce. With one phone call, the margin you planned for yourself is gone. Hijacked.

During some seasons it seems like a week doesn't pass without some sort of life event forcing us to follow a detour. And we follow it willingly, don't we, without missing a beat? We set our plans aside for our families, for our friends, for our communities. While we wouldn't have it any other way, we can adopt a better approach to rolling with those detours.

I dropped my daughter off at a family friend's house the other day so that she could go swimming with them at the aquatic center. We were chatting in my friend's kitchen for a moment, drinking tea, when she accidentally knocked her boiling hot tea directly into her lap. The last place one should go with first-degree burns is to a public swimming pool. Her day was hijacked.

My sister was running late for the baby shower she was cohosting when an old watermelon literally exploded on her kitchen counter. I didn't know watermelons could do that. Apparently, if they're old enough, they can. It was a disgusting rotten mess. Hijacked.

Being busy well doesn't mean finally figuring out how to keep our calendars from getting hijacked. Wouldn't that be nice? But trying to outsmart life's unexpected circumstances or anticipate every detour will leave you even more mentally drained and overextended than succumbing to it. Being busy well involves leaning into those turns and carrying with you the grace to roll with it.

It's like battling large waves on a shore. When the water of Lake Michigan isn't a blistery 50 degrees, my kids and I love to play in the waves. We've learned that the water is most enjoyable when the flag flying that day is yellow. When a green flag is flying, the waves are practically nonexistent. *Boring.* And when it's red, we stay the heck out of them. But we've found yellow to be where the fun lies. Diving headfirst directly into the waves as they roll in is so much fun.

What *isn't* always so fun is trying to outrun, fight, or avoid getting blasted by the larger waves. Even worse is when you aren't paying attention and you get blindsided by one. That's one way to come up gasping for air with a bathing suit full of sand.

Instead of staying out of the waves altogether or working overtime to outrun them all, we can lean into them, expect them, and even have fun with them. But how exactly do we do that? Through two practices that I like to call under-committing and bubble-wrapping our busy seasons.

UNDER-COMMITTING

When it comes to the cost of a home renovation or vacation, I tend to be an overestimator. I assume it's going to cost way more than it will, and then I'm pleasantly surprised when it turns out to be cheaper.

Bam. It's like I made money. My husband, on the other hand, does the opposite.

> HIM: "We should be able to get the house painted for about $500, don't ya think?"
>
> ME: "I mean, yeah, maybe . . . if we hire our daughter's seventh-grade class to paint it."

When it comes to time-related activities, however, I notoriously *underestimate* how long something is going to take and assume I can accomplish so much more than is actually possible during a limited amount of time. In fact, many of us do. It's known as the *planning fallacy.*

The planning fallacy is what is called "a cognitive bias." Daniel Kahneman and Amos Tversky define the planning fallacy as "the tendency to underestimate the amount of time needed to complete a future task, due in part to the reliance on overly optimistic performance scenarios." While I wouldn't characterize myself as an "overly optimistic" individual, when it comes to the number of things I believe I can accomplish in a given amount of time, I become quite overzealous.

The planning fallacy takes advantage of our unruly ambition, causing us to willingly commit to more things than we can handle. The next thing you know, you're looking at a schedule so packed you don't even have wiggle room left for, say, your littlest to use the restroom. You end up with a figurative bathing suit full of sand, a handful of half-completed tasks, a fridge full of food you don't have time to cook, and no mental energy left to be present for this season.

In order to avoid this rather uncomfortable way of life, we must practice the art of under-committing. This means, in essence, biting off even less than we think we can chew.

It's safe to assume that we've all found ourselves committing to something when we have lots of energy, only to find ourselves asking,

"What was I thinking?!" when it comes time to execute. What if we start thinking ahead? It's time to take a lesson from the pages of our own history book and realize we likely have less capacity than we think we do.

Through the practice of under-committing, we can set ourselves up for success. It's far easier to add in a last-minute social event or volunteer to help someone out of a bind on a dime when we've left margin in our calendar. When excessively busy, we don't have time for even small moments of generosity. Heck, I barely have time for eye contact. I find myself walking quickly, with my head down, avoiding eye contact at school pickup because even one thirty-second conversation is enough of a delay to force a derailment. Under-booking your calendar can help accommodate schedule hijackings and leave you with the capacity to even embrace them.

On top of causing us to overcommit, the planning fallacy also causes us to *under*estimate how much time we need to recover between our busier seasons.

BUBBLE-WRAP YOUR BUSY SEASONS

In preparation for our move, I ordered a giant roll of bubble wrap so that we'd be able to safely transport our dishes and glassware across town. As you know, cramming as much glassware in a box as possible without a proper layer of bubble wrap is a terrible packing strategy. You'd never do that, seal it shut, and then send it off with a moving company. (Unless it were something like, say, your wife's collection of vintage coffee mugs you were secretly hoping would break during transportation. *Don't even think about it, Paul.*) Instead, you'd carefully wrap each one with a hefty layer of air-filled plastic to ensure their safe arrival. Without bubble wrap, fragile items are likely to arrive at their destination in pieces. This is how we should be treating our capacity following each busy season: like the valuable and irreplaceable artifact it is.

One of the most important habits to develop as you move in and out of busy seasons is the practice of "bubble-wrapping" your busy seasons with plenty of margin. Margin is to your capacity what bubble wrap is to those vintage coffee mugs: a safeguard to ensure you arrive in one piece.

While keeping moments of margin *within* your busy schedule is vital, and while under-committing helps you better adjust to unforeseen circumstances, those strategies alone won't replenish your capacity. The best method for ensuring you get to feel like a person instead of just a self-driving vehicle is to surround chaotic seasons with days, weeks, or even an entire season of down time, if at all possible. You need margin on both sides of busy. When a busy season has been properly bubble-wrapped, it's far easier to be present within chaos, because you know you have that bubble wrap to rely on. It promises both a fresh start and reprieve on the horizon, so you don't have to worry so much about finding the air pockets for survival.

My only saving grace during this crazy busy week is knowing I've properly bubble-wrapped it. I'm looking forward to a nice chunk of margin ahead of me in T minus two days. Because of that, and only that, I am able to remain present during this week and still make progress toward my writing goal.

Without the bubble wrap, we can't afford to let our guard down long enough to enjoy the moment. Instead, we shift from busy to hurry. That's when things start to fall apart and kids get left standing on the sidewalk as you drive away from school, thinking they'd gotten in the car with you. *Whoopsie.*

Think of it like baking muffins or boiling water. If you fill the muffin tins or the pot of water to just below the brim, they're going to overflow as the temperature rises. While I do love a big ole' crispy muffin top, boiling pasta water all over the stove top is a mess to clean. You've got to leave room for things to rise.

If this were a Goldilocks situation, we'd actually want to *avoid* choosing the bed that fits just right. Because it'll only fit just right for a short time. Instead, we want to opt for the one that offers plenty of space in which to move around.

EXPERIENCING RESISTANCE

It sounds easy enough, but the moment you start to push back against the temptation to fill your schedule and operate above capacity, you'll experience resistance. Perhaps family, colleagues, supervisors, or friends have grown used to your willingness to take on more than you can handle. Or maybe it's you: you overcommit out of guilt, to avoid pain, or to stay ahead of the game. It's not easy to hold weekends and evenings free when you're asked to help out, take on a new commitment, or make more plans. Saying no can leave you feeling selfish. After all, you've got it easy compared to others. Because of that, you feel as though you *should* have the capacity for this.

The fear of missing out is another reason we fail to properly bubble-wrap hectic seasons. Maybe the thought of you or your kids missing out on fun activities or unique opportunities makes you crazy. You'd rather run yourself into the ground than get left behind. I get it. It's hard to protect your margin when nobody else seems to care about theirs. Yet if you want to create more margin, you're going to have to make choices nobody else is making. And that starts by safeguarding the space for the meaningful activities you care about and periods of rest you desperately need.

Another common reason we experience margin deprivation is habit. We've gotten so used to running on empty that allowing ourselves the free time to recover feels like opulence. We've grown used to living in survival mode, escaping one busy season just to immediately jump into another one. In order to move away from our chronic overcommitment, we need a commitment detox.

I'm not suggesting you force your high schooler to take a season off from varsity sports. But I want you to look ahead at your calendar and identify areas where you can lay down some serious bubble wrap. Go ahead and cross off weekends, evenings, or an entire season to provide yourself with a chance to recoup. I mean really recoup—not just take a big deep breath but allow yourself enough time to bring your heart rate back to baseline for an extended period.

For example, years ago I coached fall and spring soccer. It was great until it wasn't. Eventually, it started to feel as though the fall season started approximately thirty seconds after the spring season ended. I started dreading the beginning of every soccer season instead of being excited to coach, like I used to be. I didn't need to find a better soccer coaching strategy or quit my job to coach youth soccer pro bono full time. No. What I needed was more time in between this time-consuming and energy-draining commitment. Opting to forgo spring soccer was the greatest gift I've given myself, my family, and my team. Not only did it provide me and my family with more margin; it gave other players a chance to try new sports like golf and baseball without overbooking their own calendars.

Being busy well means ensuring we're starting out with a full cup when we enter a new season. To do that, we've got to properly bubble-wrap the time surrounding those busy seasons while under-committing within them.

Once we start almost expecting our plans to get hijacked and our soup to turn to soap, we'll find it far easier to be present and accommodating of those forced changes in plans. Instead of seeing those plans as adding to our workload, we can learn to confidently let the less important things fall to the wayside when life adds more to our plate than we can carry at one time.

It's hard, though, because we don't typically look at letting go, drop-ping the ball, or quitting as a strategy for success. Quitting is viewed as a failure, the result of being someone who simply can't hack it.

In a world that credits hustle and stick-to-it-iveness as defining characteristics of winners, it can be terribly difficult to walk away from things, even when those things aren't working. But part of being busy well means we're willing to toss in the towel for the sake of our sanity.

TIP FOR BEING BUSY WELL:
BATCH BORING

Batching is a time-management and productivity strategy that has been around for ages. If you've ever read a time-management book, you've likely already heard of it. If not, I'll explain. Batching is the practice of compiling like tasks and then tackling them all at once. Rather than hopping around from phone calls to emails to housework to creative work, you assemble similar tasks and get them all done in the same set period of time.

Monday mornings are my designated boring-tasks days. I have Monday off, so I use the morning to put my home in order, run errands, make appointments, finalize any decisions I need to make, and brain dump for the week. (You can find a brain dump template on p. 182.) I look at it as a "get crap done" day.

While meaningful moments can't be batched, the boring stuff can. In fact, batching the boring stuff leaves us with more margin for the things that matter most to us.

If you're prone to procrastinating on mundane tasks until they become urgent, try batching boring to get it all done at once.

CHAPTER SIX

Be a Quitter
The Art of Walking Away

Whether it's a dinner recipe, tradition, friendship, favorite restaurant, or place of employment, I'm as loyal as they come. It takes an incredible amount of convincing for me to quit something. I spent eleven years as a labor and delivery nurse before calling it quits to stay home full-time with my babies for a season. When I finally pulled the trigger and had that awkward conversation with my boss, she wasn't at all surprised, and my friends and family responded with, "*Finally.* It's about time." They could see my next right step long before I could. It was a decision I had been wrestling with, a fact apparently obvious to everyone but me.

While loyalty can be a positive character trait, it can easily morph into a flaw. Ever heard the phrase "loyal to a fault"? We can become so committed to our opinions that we fail to grow. We can remain loyal to a family tradition even though it has become a stressful event rather than a joyful point of connection. We can hang on to unhealthy coping strategies and habits because—well, they've gotten us this far, haven't they?

When it comes to our schedules, loyalty can keep us committed to tasks and responsibilities for which we no longer have capacity. Instead of pausing them for a season or permanently passing the baton, we keep showing up and allocating our most precious resources—time, attention, and energy—to a commitment that has run its course.

Our ability to create and maintain margin in our lives is directly proportional to our willingness to quit activities that are no longer working. For many of us, though, the thought of quitting is absurd. The very act of walking away leaves us feeling like we lack the grit to see it through.

But for some activities, that's just not the case. In fact, quitting very well may be the grittiest thing you can do.

TAPPING OUT

In 2015, the History Channel launched the popular TV series *Alone*. In it, ten contestants get dropped off, alone, in the harsh wilderness for an undetermined amount of time. They are only allowed to take along ten survival items, chosen from a preapproved list of forty items. Whoever survives the longest without tapping out wins half a million dollars. There are no camera crews to accompany them. Instead, contestants are given video equipment to lug around and are charged with the task of recording their own experiences. To top it off, they are strategically placed with roughly ten miles between each contestant to ensure they are *alone*, alone. The only contact they have with the outside world throughout the entire show are regular health and weight checks. But that's it.

One episode, in particular, has stood out to me more than any other. I don't want to share any spoilers, so I'll just tell you it occurs in season three. During this episode, one contestant opts to tap out. All things considered, he is doing well, and he has even built himself an impressive shelter. Throughout this particular episode, we witness his struggle to decide whether to stick it out or tap out.

When he finally makes the call to go home, he shares these words to explain the reasoning behind his decision to call it quits. He says, quite simply but profoundly, "I'm not really tapping out; I'm tapping back in to my life at home." He was done missing out on the things that mattered the most to him.

Everything comes with an exchange. Everything. Every single yes comes at the loss of something in its place. Saying yes to a promotion may come with more time-consuming responsibilities that will pull you away from home. Saying yes to coaching youth sports will inevitably eat up your evenings, weekends, and a surprising amount of your mental energy. And volunteering to participate in a survival show could leave you missing weeks or even months at home with your family. Every single yes comes with some sort of sacrifice, whether big or small.

Positive habits come at a cost as well. If you opt to start an early-morning workout routine, you're going to sacrifice sleep. If you choose to declutter your home and live with less, it's going to take time, effort, and a commitment to ignore trends.

In the same way, tapping out, saying no, and under-committing come with a cost. The difference, however, is that tapping out *creates* margin while saying yes *consumes* it. Tapping out can open the door for seasons of rest and time for deeper connection with those we love. It can also leave space for us to say yes to exciting new opportunities we never saw coming.

THE POWER OF QUITTING

Ina Garten wasn't always the Barefoot Contessa. Prior to becoming a beloved Food Network chef, she worked at the White House, where she helped write nuclear energy budgets under presidents Ford and Carter. (I know, I had no idea either.)

When she was thirty years old, she started to second-guess her career choice. Ina Garten started teaching herself how to cook by working her way through Julia Child's cookbook. Eventually, with the encouragement of her devoted husband, Jeffrey, Ina Garten quit her job in DC and bought a specialty food store in West Hampton Beach, New York—a town she'd never even been to before. The name of that store? The Barefoot Contessa. Little did she know that twenty-plus years later, her beloved, Emmy-winning cooking show, *The Barefoot Contessa*, would debut. The rest is history.

Ina's success story isn't unique. Well, her whole rise to stardom thing may be, but you can find countless variations of similar before and after stories. Bob Goff, founder of Love Does, honorary consul to the Republic of Uganda, and author of multiple *New York Times* bestselling books, used to own his own law firm. One day, on something of a whim, he quit. He quit his *own* law firm.

In fact, Goff quits something every Thursday. He writes:

> I was *so* busy and my life was *so* full that I started to worry I was doing a lot of different things, but some of those things didn't really matter. I needed to make a big change in my life so I had room for the important stuff. I decided to declare Thursdays as "Quit Something Day." I quit one thing every Thursday. I'm not kidding! I quit things like helping lead an organization or complaining or eating marshmallows. It could be anything! I even quit my job on Thursday. I started to realize that in order to have time for the most important things in my life, I needed to be willing to let go of a lot of other things.

Yet the concept of quitting holds negative connotations. We assume it's for people who don't have the willpower or stamina to finish strong. As the popular saying goes, "Winners never quit, and quitters never win."

Goff and Garten would likely disagree with that statement. What if Ina Garten hadn't quit her government job? We might never have her Perfect Roast Chicken recipe. If Bob Goff hadn't quit his own law firm, the Love Does foundation may not have gone on to build as many schools as it has.

Now, I may not be a Food Network star like Garten or honorary consul to another country like Goff. But if I hadn't quit my labor and delivery job, I might never have authored a single book or been available to take on the job of school nurse at my kids' school during the pandemic. I might never have stumbled across the concept of minimalism at all and might still be drowning in kitchen appliances, excess bedsheets, and laundry. Quitters win all the time when they quit the right things. Sometimes we've got to tap out of one thing so we can tap in to another.

Quitting can be just as much of a gift as seeing things through can be. Some things just aren't worth the cost they require. Perhaps it's not your job or the company you founded you need to quit. In fact, typically it's the smaller tasks and commitments we won't let go of that clutter up our calendar, keeping us overextended, distracted, and unavailable.

Quitting gives us margin to find gratitude as well. When we're running nonstop, it's easy to see our full calendars as a burden rather than a blessing. Margin affords us a minute to align our focus on this one truth: there is always something to be grateful for in every season.

When we are margin-deprived, we have little to no capacity for spontaneous moments of generosity. We don't have the wiggle room to drive a kid's classmate home from school, make a meal for a friend who could use some help, or take the time to chat with our vintage neighbor. ("Eighty-three isn't elderly," my neighbor tells me, "It's vintage.")

When it comes to living a meaningful life, margin is a must.

YOU CAN QUIT THAT

I used to make homemade peanut butter. It was delicious and not all that complicated, but man, did it make a huge mess. On top of that, we'd frequently run out of peanut butter (something my family eats regularly), and rather than pick some up at the grocery store like a normal person, I'd have to be extra and make it myself.

The longer I made peanut butter, the less motivated I became to make it. But to me, it was a task I had started and therefore committed to. For life.

One day, while I was begrudgingly grinding peanuts into butter, my husband walked through the kitchen and read the label on the package of honey-roasted peanuts I used. "This isn't even healthier!" he said in shock.

As he read the label to me, we realized my peanut better actually had more sugar and unhealthy fats in it than a jar of store-bought peanut butter did. No wonder it was so flipping delicious. I had just assumed all my effort made it the healthier option. On top of that, the cost savings was negligible at best.

Shortly after that, I tossed in the towel on my peanut-butter making days (the many, many literal towels that cleaning up this mess required).

It's funny what quitting one little task can do for you. Quitting this one, while simple, left me evaluating how I used my time from every angle. I was now on the hunt for any other lifetime commitments I'd inadvertently made, and I started quitting any of them I could. I ditched bigger commitments, like coaching spring soccer, all the way down to the smaller tasks, like turning our clothes right-side-out before folding them. That simple but effective move cut my laundry folding time in almost half. Who would have thought?

ON QUITTING TRADITIONS

I used to view keeping holiday and family traditions as my personal responsibility. After all, I am the oldest child. We tend to believe our family traditions must look the same year after year until death do us part. (Don't think you're changing the order of Christmas Day on us—not on our watch!) But just as seasons change, children age, and people evolve, so can the way we do just about everything. Letting go of expectations can allow us to enjoy each holiday so much more. Instead of putting on a production, we get to participate. You don't have to take on the role of family tradition choreographer any longer. Instead, you can take a seat in the audience and let the holidays unfold as they will. The byproduct may look a little messy, but in my experience, it's far more enjoyable.

I'm Lebanese, but I didn't grow up eating chicken shawarma. When people I meet learn that I love to cook Lebanese food, they always ask me, "Ooooh, do you know how to make chicken shawarma?" Unfortunately, though, I don't have a family recipe for that one. My grandma, who taught me how to cook our family's most beloved dishes, never made it, and therefore I never learned how. I assumed there was some geographical reason. Perhaps chicken shawarma just wasn't a popular dish in the region of Lebanon where my grandma was born.

One day, I thought to ask her. "Teta, how come we never had chicken shawarma growing up? I don't recall you ever making it."

She smiled and replied simply, "I don't like it."

That's it. There wasn't a complicated reason, and it had nothing to do with geography or ancestry. She never cooked chicken shawarma because she didn't like chicken shawarma.

Some of these traditions we keep have little to do with what we want to do and everything to do with what worked well for previous generations. If you no longer care to orchestrate elaborate holiday traditions, it's okay to stop doing that. Or if those traditions simply aren't working during the chaotic season of life you're in, it's okay to pause them. You can always pick them back up when the timing is right.

I used to think traditions could only be called "traditions" if executed with precision and consistency. Once established, they should be repeated every year for all of eternity. Amen. That's just not true.

Just as sentiment or memories aren't locked inside a family heirloom or souvenir, neither is tradition beholden to the activity itself. Tradition, memories, and sentiment are found in experiencing connection. The activity is simply the vehicle. Holiday traditions don't need to occur the exact same way, every single year. The joy isn't contingent upon what you're able to squeeze in, check off, or experience.

Many of us have been putting a lot of unnecessary pressure on ourselves, and we're the ones who pay the highest price for it. We miss out on experiencing the joy in the everyday moments when we're too distracted by all the should-do's and have-to-do's.

My little family didn't get around to carving pumpkins this year. That's something we've done every single year. Between Raegan's theater production, Jameson's concussion appointments, my book deadline, and packing for our move, there simply was no time for pumpkin carving. Something had to give. While I did feel bad that we couldn't make it happen, it gave me a chance to talk to my kids about capacity.

We can't always do all the things, and it's important our kids learn that about us and themselves as well. In the long run, quitting, pausing, and regularly reevaluating traditions just may be the most important tradition you can adopt.

SUNK COST BIAS

I've got a friend with an extreme phobia of moths. (You know who you are.) If a moth were to come anywhere near her, she'd shove you in front of a bus to get away from it. Wouldn't blink an eye. She goes into fight-or-flight mode at the mere sight of the smallest moth on the other side of the room.

Margin deprivation tends to send us into a similar fight-or-flight mode. We start snapping at the very ones we're busy *for*. We forget what a gift it is to even have a job that allows us to feed our families, let alone allows our kids to participate in extracurricular activities. We curse at the inconvenience of traffic jams and begin to resent the activities we signed our own family up for. These are activities we'd probably enjoy if it we weren't sputtering through our overly tight schedules with our capacity flashing empty. Yet even so, we press on. We continue living hurriedly, both depleted and overstimulated. It can be due to something as obvious as pride or as subtle as a lack of confidence. We might stick with something far longer than we should out of obligation or a fear of missing out.

Another common contributor to our unwillingness to quit is something called *sunk cost bias*. In fact, it may be the most influential one of all. Sunk cost bias is our tendency to stick with something because we've already invested so much into it. We may hold on to a sweater because of how much it cost. Or maybe we stick with a commitment simply because we've already been at it for so many years. Whether it be money, time, or energy, the more we've invested, the less likely we are to walk away.

I love to read. One thing I started doing in recent years is leaving books unfinished. *Gasp.* I used to *have* to finish a book. Obviously, nobody was forcing this on me, but my own brain said, "Once you've read the first chapter, it's imperative that you see this book to the end." If winners never quit, then readers never leave a book unfinished.

Now, however, sometimes I'll get as far as 120 pages into a book—and walk away. Without hesitation. If a novel isn't keeping my interest or a nonfiction book isn't adding value to my life, there's no sense in pressing on. There are just too many books in the sea to keep reading what you aren't enjoying. In fact, I don't even hold on to a book that loses my interest just in case I change my mind. Instead, I confidently return it to the library or donate it if it's a book I had purchased.

Sunk cost bias says: "Well, you bought the book, so you need to read it." Or: "You've already devoted so much time to reading the first one hundred pages, you have to finish the last one hundred to make that time spent count for *some*thing."

I say: "Heck, if this book isn't doing it for you, walk away. No hard feelings."

We've got to stop looking at traditions, commitments, tasks, habits, and completed books like monuments to our accomplishments. What isn't working? What has run its course? What can you quit doing so you can free up your irreplaceable time, attention, and energy for more enjoyable and purposeful tasks? Sure, quitting some commitments *can* be a bad thing. But when used wisely, with sincere intention, quitting can be an incredibly beneficial tool for preventing hurried living.

QUITTING WHAT *IS* WORKING

Quitting a task that is no longer serving you is hard. Yet, quitting the things that are working well is even harder. During the seasons of life when busyness is just flat out unavoidable, you may find you also need to go ahead and quit things that *are* working. Even if just for that season.

Maybe you've got a meal plan that saves your life during busier seasons. Yet right now, during this week, it's still too much to manage. Perhaps you love to sign up to help during classroom parties, chaperone field trips, or volunteer in your church's children's ministry on Sunday morning, but during the next couple of months, you know you're going to be drowning.

Sometimes even beneficial habits like your early-morning workout routine will need to move to the back burner, because this week you've got to drive your son to soccer conditioning at the crack of dawn. While you likely won't find *that* bit of advice on the pages of top-selling time-management books, it's true, isn't it? It's what we do for our kids without blinking an eye. We let our own workout routines sit on the bench so they don't have to. Or we drop what we're working on when a friend needs a hand, or we miss our morning run for the well-child pediatrician visit that took us six months to get. While regular exercise is incredibly important, there are times when it's simply out of reach. Instead of now rising at 4 a.m. to fit it in or beating yourself up over it all week, lean into it and know it's a sacrifice you've chosen to make on purpose, just for a season.

Remember that quitting something doesn't have to be permanent. We need to hold to our nos just as loosely as we do to our yesses. Maybe for the next class party, you don't sign up to bring something. Or you wait until after your move to resume volunteering at church on Sunday morning. Pausing can be just as effective as quitting altogether.

Regardless of whether you end up quitting that task for a moment or for good, pulling the plug can be flat out hard. But when we know we're tapping out in order to tap *in* to something else, we can proceed with confidence. When life's pace picks up steam, instead of asking, "How am I going to pull this off?" start asking yourself, "What do I need to quit right now?"

If you're having a hard time figuring out exactly what you can let go of, consider asking a friend or your partner. They often have a more objective vantage point than you do. It can be easier for them to see the things taking up too much time unnecessarily. Quitting will get easier the more you practice doing it. But if you're having a hard time finding the right words, it's time to learn how to say no.

TIP FOR BEING BUSY WELL:
QUIT SMALL

Keep in mind that the things you choose to quit don't need to be big tasks or major time savers. When decluttering for the first time, I encourage people to start in the smaller, more insignificant areas of their homes first. It helps develop your decluttering IQ, so to speak. We should do the same thing as we start to quit commitments as well. Bob Goff didn't quit his law firm on his first "quit something" Thursday. No, that leap came much later, *after* he'd had lots of practice eliminating simpler tasks.

Look around for the ways you've been making peanut butter for no good reason at all. Quit something small, like turning your kids' clothes right-side-out before folding them. Or, better yet, if age appropriate, quit folding your kids' clothes for them altogether. It's easy to continue taking on tasks for our kids even after they've grown capable of doing it themselves. If you're caring for children at home, take some time today to reevaluate your to-do list, and offload any chores your kids can take on themselves.

CHAPTER SEVEN

Be Rude
The Art of Saying No

Years ago, my husband and I swung by his sweet Grandma Sally's house one afternoon to make dinner plans with her. Paul and I didn't have any kids at the time, but we worked opposite shifts, which added an element of difficulty when making any sort of plans. We proposed an evening, and Grandma Sally pulled her bird-themed calendar off the wall to see if it suited her.

"Oh no, that won't work," she said. "I have an appointment that morning at JC Penney to order some curtains."

Paul and I subtly locked side-eyes. As twentysomethings, we were both thinking the exact same thing. *She can't go to dinner with us because she has an 11 a.m. appointment to pick out curtains?!*

We found another date and laughed it off later, assuming Grandma Sally just couldn't hang like she once could. But now, years later, I've grown to appreciate the intentionality and confidence with which Grandma Sally made plans that day.

For many of us, saying no to requests or plans can be difficult. Why, though? Why are we so afraid to say it like it is? What keeps us from treating our time with the intentionality and care it deserves? Sure, it could be something complex: previous generations modeling overcommitment and expecting the same in return, or our hesitation to appear rude, or our internal fear of rejection. These underlying factors are certainly important to address.

But it might not be all that complicated. Maybe we just don't feel equipped with the right words to decline invitations and requests. When put on the spot, it's easy to succumb to overcommitment simply because we don't know how to decline in a timely and decisive manner.

So if "Sure, I can make that work," has always been your default response, it's time to risk being a little rude.

WWGSD? (WHAT WOULD GRANDMA SALLY DO?)

Instead of begrudgingly saying yes or dodging phone calls to prevent ourselves from being asked in the first place, we can take a few lessons from how Grandma Sally avoided overfilling her dance card.

If you're ready to create a calendar that fits your real life, you're going to have to venture into uncharted territory. And you'll have to do it with the confidence of an eighty-year-old grandmother.

1. Assess Your Capacity over Your Calendar

If Grandma Sally was simply evaluating her availability as it pertained to *time*, then by all means she would have said yes. There was plenty of actual time in her day for a trip to JC Penney *and* dinner. After all, she was still going to have to eat.

But she wasn't looking at time; she was assessing her capacity. Only assessing our actual, literal, physical availability is a surefire way to land ourselves in a state of hurry. At first glance, the day may seem wide open. Yet when we fail to consider our current energy levels, the pace we had to maintain for the last few days, or what lies ahead, it's only a matter of time before we're running on empty. Grandma Sally was likely bubble-wrapping her trip to JC Penney, because choosing things like curtains and paint colors can be remarkably draining if it's not your forte.

2. Guard Your Calendar—Unapologetically

Grandma Sally didn't miss a beat when telling us no. She didn't say, "Let me think about it," or "Maybe I can make that work." She didn't hem and haw or even try to justify her no. She felt no need to explain why having two appointments on the same day wouldn't work for her. Eighty-year-old grandmas rarely do. That day, she simply put the saying "No is a complete sentence" into practice.

We can do the same. If you've been in the habit of feeling guilty when you turn down a request or decline an invitation even when your calendar appears bare, this will be an adjustment at first. I know the feeling. But keep at it. In time, that guilt will start to morph into confidence as you experience the benefits of maintaining margin and prioritizing your energy levels over appeasing others. Besides, most people will understand what it is you're safeguarding. In fact, you may empower them to start doing the same.

3. Prioritize the Things That Matter by Giving Them Margin

Knowing Grandma Sally, I think she just wanted to make sure she'd be in the best position to enjoy her time with her favorite grandkids. (Our words, not hers.) She didn't want to run the risk of feeling hurried, tired, or overwhelmed. This would have been a dinner she was excited for. Because of that, she wanted to show up for it fully available, attentive, and present.

Spacing out our commitments, when we can, will ensure that our time doesn't feel crammed. That way, we can be fully present. When we're tight on either time or capacity, we increase our chances of being distracted, fatigued, and hurried. That's no way to treat the things we care so deeply about.

4. Know Your Limits

Your limits depend on things like your personality type, workload, physical health, family responsibilities, and plenty of other factors. With each new season comes new limitations. Depending on where you're at, they may feel more or less restricting than the previous season.

Know yourself and how much you can take. Don't be afraid to say no because you think you *should* be capable of handling more. That mom you run into at school pickup who seems to have it all together, effortlessly prancing around the city from one thing to another without so much as a messy bun? You probably don't have the same limits. You don't know what kind of support she has or whether she's melting down at the end of the day. Or perhaps she's just significantly more extroverted than you and needs far less downtime than you do to function well. The world needs a variety of individuals. Your job isn't to show up for her life but for yours.

DISNEY PEOPLE

There are two types of people: Disney people and the rest of us. If you're not a Disney person, odds are good you know one. They tend to vacation there often, sometimes even without bringing their children along.

We are not Disney people. But we did have the luxury a few years back of taking a trip to Disney *with* Disney people. It's the best of both worlds, really. You don't have to be a fanatic, but you get to draft off their Disney know-how.

These people knew all the ins and outs of booking rides, making dining reservations, and finding cost-effective accommodations. So when they invited us to join them, saying, "Let's go in September because it tends to be a slower season," I believed them.

What I quickly learned, though, as I walked toe to heel with other Disney-goers on that hot September day, is that a Disney person's definition of "slow season" and mine are two entirely different things. I pictured nonexistent lines and photos clear of other guests. What you get, though, is maybe a two-hour wait instead of a three-hour wait. While the latter is far worse, both are awful.

The reality is that what feels like a busy season to you may feel easy-peasy to someone else, and vice versa.

More than just the quantity of tasks on your to-do list, the quality of them has an impact on your capacity as well. You may enjoy spending all day at your daughter's volleyball tournament, talking with other parents and eating concession snacks for lunch. To another parent, it's a nightmare. Yes, they may love watching their own child participate in something they're passionate about, but it's too much peopling for their capacity. What fills one person up will drain another.

Perhaps picking out curtains and grabbing dinner with family feels like margin to you but feels overwhelmingly hurried to someone else. Some people can tolerate fuller calendars, more social interaction, and a faster-paced lifestyle than others can. There is no correct number of appointments, no appropriate amount of social events, and no universal formula for living a meaningful life.

Grandma Sally knew how much she could handle in a given day, and she scheduled her time accordingly. It's time we start to do the same. We get ourselves into trouble when we assume we should have the same capacity as someone else or even the same capacity as we ourselves did, years ago. While I used to be able to work the night shift, take a nap, and then hit the gym in my twenties, just thinking about that schedule now makes me feel nauseated and exhausted. Learn your limits, assess your capacity within each new season, identify what matters most to you, and then defend a schedule that fits at all costs.

HOW TO SAY NO

If you've read *Messy Minimalism*, then you may already know my strategy for saying no. Even if you have, don't skip this section. It's worth reading again. Just this weekend, a friend texted me to ask, "What's that line you use to say no? You know, when you don't have the energy for another commitment?"

It's a good one, so listen up: "Sorry, I can't. I don't have the capacity for that right now."

It's foolproof. Nobody can argue with your capacity. I've said this to friends, school administration, coworkers, teachers, and church leaders. Heck, I've even used it on my own kids and husband before when they ask me to do one more thing while I'm already drowning. Capacity is a far more critical component of managing our time than our physical availability, yet we often overlook it. Just because you can't quantify something doesn't mean it doesn't exist or it isn't important. Capacity is actually the *most* important thing to evaluate.

Why? Because time can be flexible. Your calendar may be full in the evening, but what about the afternoon? Oh, tonight doesn't work? What about tomorrow? Capacity, however, can't pivot nearly as easily. Although basketball season, and all that comes with it, may end abruptly following a tournament, your capacity is going to take more time to recover. While you may now be able to see more free time in your calendar, only you can know when your capacity will be available again.

LEARNING THE HARD WAY

My son was eight years old when he first went hunting with his grandpa. I had never been hunting before either, and so I opted to tag along. I woke my son up well before dawn, got us both dressed in multiple layers, and headed to meet up with my dad. He was waiting for us when we arrived, gear in hand and ready to hike to our blind in the woods.

We had gotten out of the car and were walking toward him when, on this pitch-black winter morning, my dad suddenly whipped his head in my direction and looked at me in shock. His jaw was practically on the ground, and I had no idea why.

"What?" I responded nervously.

Silently staring at me in disbelief, he slowly pointed, as if it should be obvious to me, down to the light-up Ninja Turtle boots my son was wearing. That's right, I had dressed my son in his bright, flashing, light-up boots—to go hunting. His every move illuminated the night sky. My dad tried to remedy the situation with duct tape. But those bright little feet still lit up our hunting blind like a warning beacon for any deer who may have dared to come our way.

Needless to say, we didn't see any deer that morning. Lesson learned.

Anytime we take on new challenges or try new things, they always come with a learning curve. We make mistakes, show up ill-prepared, and learn as we go. It's just part of life.

I've practiced saying no so often that it's now my initial reaction to any invitation. Sometimes to a fault. "Nope!" I'll say before pausing to realize, "Oh wait . . . actually, I think I will." But this wasn't always the case. My default response was always "Sure." Changing that took time, patience, and lots of practice. The only way you'll get more comfortable and confident declining invitations is by being willing to be a total amateur at it at first.

As you start to dabble with declining invitations and commitments, you'll get it wrong now and then. You'll say yes and regret it. You'll say no and maybe later wish you hadn't. That's okay. Practice isn't meant to make us perfect; it's meant to help us develop sustainable habits. Instead of struggling to make the perfect decision, start letting no become your go-to response. Just for a season. Doing this will help break the habit of overcommitment and establish the muscle memory to say no with greater confidence in the future. Besides, if you're going to err, let it be on the side of under-committing rather than overcommitting. You can take back a no far easier than you can a yes.

BEING GENEROUS WITH YOUR TIME

I really don't enjoy public speaking. I do it, and afterward I'm always glad I did, but the days leading up to it tend to suck the life out of me. Even just writing that about public speaking has made my palms instantly sweaty.

Small, local moms groups are the exception, though, because I first found minimalism in a moms group. That's where everything changed for me. Speaking to a group of moms feels like an opportunity to pass along the same life preserver that was tossed to me years ago.

During my most recent speaking engagement, one young mother raised her hand during the Q&A portion of my talk and asked this beautiful question about time management: "But isn't saying no not being generous with our time like we're called to?"

What a great, honest, and difficult question! Isn't that how many of us feel? If we believe that we are created to live in community and to serve one another in love, then saying no is the very opposite of that, right? If saying yes is having a servant's heart, then saying no must be selfish.

The missing piece here is this: we were each created with unique gifts and a limited capacity. Remember that every decision comes with an exchange. There is absolutely a time and place to sacrifice your capacity on the altar of generosity. Like that time my sister Renee stayed with me in the hospital when Amelia was in the ICU with respiratory syncytial virus (RSV) at just three months old. Paul was holding down the fort at home, caring for our two other anxious little ones, and I had been up for nearly forty-eight hours. By this time, I was so tired I could hardly form a complete sentence. Renee came to my aid, allowing me to pass out in the recliner while she stayed awake all night giving Amelia her pacifier everytime she fussed—which was often, as she also struggled to sleep while connected to all those tubes and wires.

Renee's time generosity was the greatest gift our family could receive that night. But remember: there is only so much of you to go around. One can't function with that level of generosity every single day. It's important to pull away for moments and seasons in order to fill back up and be a person. When we devote ourselves to too many tasks, we won't have the capacity to step in when we are desperately needed.

While it seems counterproductive, saying *no* can be just as generous a response as saying *yes*. What happens if you commit to something you don't have the capacity for? You're going to do it poorly. You're not going to be able to show up with your whole heart and give it your all. People aren't asking you for help because they need someone who can assist them halfway. When you say no, it gives them a chance to find someone with the capacity to show up all the way.

There are a variety of reasons we feel compelled to say yes when we just—can't—even. You may be afraid of letting someone down, leaving someone in a bind, or admitting you have a limit at all. Remember, we weren't created to do everything, only our things. Nobody out there has a never-ending supply of give. Everyone needs a reprieve from time to time. Take yours, unapologetically. That way, when needs arise, you'll be able to meet them fervently.

SAYING NO WHEN IT'S HARD

With just three weeks left until we moved, I wandered around the Christmas makers market at my kids' school. I bought homemade Christmas cards by Brooklyn, salsa by the Korreys, a succulent candle by Ella, and cookies by Serenity. It was fun, but the best part of all was my kids were *not* selling stuff.

Don't get me wrong. My kids had made quite a strong case for participating in this event. They even promised I "wouldn't have to do a thing to help." *Ha.* I've got well over a decade of parenting experience under my belt, so this wasn't my first rodeo. I wouldn't have to help? Who did they think they are fooling?

As I strolled up and down the aisles, admiring everyone's hard work, I was so grateful that I had said no to this commitment for our family. I had taken the time to look ahead and assess what my capacity would look like now, three weeks before our move.

With a little practice, saying no to overcommitment—even when the opportunity is fun and exciting, even when your kids are begging you to say yes—can become one of your greatest strengths. While you may start out stumbling through your *no*, like a rookie hunter wearing light-up boots in a deer blind, eventually you'll be saying no with confidence.

For some, saying no seems to come naturally. There are people out there who don't overthink every no. They don't assume the world will fall apart if they aren't the ones to take on the job. Just yesterday I asked a friend for a favor. I needed someone to coach a soccer game for me while I was out of town. My friend's response was a quick and confident: "I can't take that on right now." While it seemed like it was second nature for her, it's something I know she has worked to develop. If saying no is hard for you, don't settle for that. Work at it. Overcommitment and people-pleasing are habits worth changing.

I wasn't insulted that my friend said no, either. In fact, I was grateful she felt comfortable enough to say no. While it's hard to say no, it's often even harder to ask for help. Why? Because the last thing we want to do is put someone in a tough spot. This can lead us into a vicious spiral: feeling pressured to say yes to others, but then never asking for help ourselves for fear of putting added pressure on someone else. When you start saying no more often, you may just find it easier to ask for help when you need it as well.

You know what? I figured it out, too. I found a parent with a little more capacity that week. It wasn't my friend's job to pick up the slack; it was my job to find someone who could.

Let me restate that: it's not your job to pick up all the slack.

Saying yes when you can't afford it isn't kind to anybody. It leaves you less equipped to give the best of yourself to the things you are already committed to. If you've done it for years, it's time to stop. Living an unhurried life depends on it.

One last thing to keep in mind as you begin practicing your confident old-lady no: remember that no doesn't have to be permanent. We talked about this a bit in the last chapter. Quitting, sitting out a season, saying "No, I can't take that on right now"—these things aren't forever. They can be, if you want them to, or they can be temporary. When you move into a slower season, you'll have the option to pick back up where you left off. Just because you don't have the capacity today doesn't mean you never will again.

CRISIS AVERTED

A few summers back, my kids found a baby snapping turtle at our cottage. He was the cutest little thing, despite the fact he kept trying to chomp down on their fingers. Before I knew it, this turtle, who they affectionately named Buddy, had managed to become the world's most beloved snapping turtle, and he didn't even know it. Within the hour my kids had turned our plastic kiddie pool into an all-inclusive snapping turtle resort. He had sand, he had water, and he had sun, shade, and more worms to graze on than any snapping turtle could ever hope for. He had it all. We let him spend the weekend as our guest before ceremoniously releasing him back where he was found.

We're not pet people. Never have been. Prior to that brief forty-eight hours of snapping turtle ownership, we'd never had more than a beta fish. Watching my kids have so much fun caring for that little turtle, however, led me to consider buying them an actual pet turtle. How hard could it be?

The longer I thought about it, the more I liked this pet turtle idea. He'd be contained to a tank, and our neighbors could pop in to feed him for us when we go on vacation.

Luckily, before I pulled the trigger, a thought occurred to me. *Wait. How long do box turtles live?*

The answer? According to Google, the life expectancy of a pet turtle can be up to thirty-five years! So in theory, I could still be taking care of this pet turtle when my kids are married and having children of their own. I'd be eligible for Social Security before this turtle went to turtle heaven. *Shut it down.*

In a perfect world, we'd always catch ourselves on the front end, before we're in too deep. But that's not what happens. Whether we've accidentally overcommitted or life has simply hijacked our intentionally established margin, we're bound to find ourselves approaching hurry-level living from time to time. Instead of kicking ourselves, hustling harder, or abandoning our pet turtles on the fire station doorstep, we can put a plan in place to help us survive seasons of chaos when they occur. Instead of panicking or making it up as we go along, we can create what I've come to call a *busy protocol* to help weather the chaos of those inevitable busier seasons of life.

TIP FOR BEING BUSY WELL: SAY NO SOONER RATHER THAN LATER

Have you ever put off saying no until it feels too late? Perhaps you weren't sure you could make it work or you really didn't want to, but the thought of disappointing someone or missing out felt like too much.

Procrastinating your no doesn't do anybody any favors, though. Saying no early on gives the asker the best opportunity to come up with another plan. It also immediately relieves your mental load of the lingering question: *How am I going to get out of this?* When we put off saying no, we run the risk of feeling pressured into saying yes because we missed our chance to say no. If everything in you is screaming, *Yeah, I'm definitely not doing that,* go ahead and get it off your chest as soon as possible.

CHAPTER EIGHT

Be Proactive

The Practice of Being Ready for Anything

During nursing school, I managed to land a summer externship at our local hospital, where I was assigned to the Pediatric Outpatient Surgery Center. It was a sweet gig on a highly coveted unit, and I learned so much that summer.

My most vivid memory from this externship, however, was the day I called a code. In a hospital, a code is a message you send to an extremely skilled group of hospital staff that a patient on your unit is literally on the verge of death. Since the pediatric outpatient unit is mostly for simpler procedures like tubes and tonsillectomies, a code on our floor was highly unlikely. I mean, the unit's name says it all: *outpatient*. These kiddos go home the same day of their surgery.

It was the end of the day, and I was stripping beds and stocking rooms when the code went out over the loudspeaker: "All attending physicians. 3 South. Pediatric Outpatient Surgery." You could practically hear a collective gasp throughout the entire hospital. The nurses on my unit came running toward me and I toward them. We met in the hallway in a confused and disoriented panic. "Did you call it?" "No, I didn't call it." "Did *you* call it?" "NO!"

We only had one patient left on the unit at the time, and he was sitting up in bed, eating a popsicle.

That's when it dawned on me. I brought my hands up to my face as I do when I'm nervous. "Oh my word! I think I may have bumped it with the linen cart! I think I flipped the lid into the code button!" But it was too late: the protocol for life-or-death emergencies was in full swing. There was no way to undo it before this team arrived.

Over the course of the next few minutes, respiratory therapists, phlebotomists, nurses, anesthesia personnel, attending physicians, and administrators all flung open the doors to our unit, time and time again, and raced in. Every single individual who came through our doors had a look of determination in their eyes and preparedness in their step, as if they were thinking, *Not on my watch.*

As they individually got the message that this was, in fact, a false alarm, each of their postures transformed from battle-ready to relief before filing out of the unit. Eventually I had to face the administrators, who wanted to know exactly how this incident occurred.

Code buttons at this hospital now come equipped with easy-access plastic covers to prevent mishaps like this.

What can I say? I'm just innovative like that.

STOP, DROP, AND ROLL

I want us to start preparing for periods of busyness the same way hospital personnel prepare for codes: by establishing a protocol ahead of time. Sure, enduring an extensive family calendar, getting dinner on the table after working overtime, and helping your kids complete their homework is hardly the same thing as restarting someone's heart. Yet, the way in which we set ourselves up for success during busier seasons can look similar.

What is a busy protocol? It's a preestablished plan of action we can initiate when the going gets rough. When you read the words *stop, drop, and roll,* you know exactly what that means, right? If your clothes catch on fire, this is how you handle it. It's been ingrained in you ever since the fire department visited your elementary school class. Just like stop, drop, and roll, or Heimlich maneuver instructions, or the emergency contact information you might stick to the refrigerator for a babysitter, I want us to have a plan in place we can look to when we enter busy seasons.

Or take my good friend Aaron, who recently got his pilot's license. He shared with me an acronym for the protocol that pilots use during inflight emergencies. When things get dicey, pilots resort to the acronym ANC as protocol for properly handling situations as they arise. It stands for Aviate, Navigate, Communicate.

Aviate: Fly the plane. Basically, don't panic, be present, and respond to the emergency by flying in a way that is appropriate for your situation.

Navigate: Decide the direction you need go. Do you need to move around a storm or find a place to land? Once you've established control of your aircraft, it's time to figure out which direction you need to head.

Communicate: Once the first two steps are completed, it's then time to contact air traffic control for support and communicate the situation with your passengers.

Now, ideally, nobody would catch on fire or choke on their food. Ideally hospitals wouldn't need code buttons, pilots wouldn't encounter in-flight trouble, and you wouldn't need a busy protocol. But we don't live in the land of ideally, do we? Reality has proven to us time and time again that we will, in fact, endure the occasional season of busyness. No amount of simplifying—I'm talking realistic, sustainable, and attainable simplicity—will result in a permanent life of ease. We can stop adding insult to injury by pursuing a goal we can never obtain.

Instead, we can create a life we love and lean into the variability that accompanies being human. We no longer need to seek out the perfect time-blocking plan or organizational system. Sure, let simplicity do its thing, but also remember that busy is inevitable. Instead of letting a full calendar send us into a tailspin, undo our progress, derail our joy, and drain us of every last drop of gratitude, we can create and implement an emergency protocol to help us not only endure those fast-paced and exhausting seasons but fully enjoy them as well.

Simply put, life gets heavy from time to time. A busy protocol will help you respond confidently. It will assist you in offloading some of the weight while ensuring you have the strength to carry what's left.

HURRY PREVENTION

As a worst-case-scenario person, I've got a protocol for just about everything. You won't find them neatly arranged in a three-ring binder or anything. These plans exist solely in my brain. But they're there, I assure you.

I've got a mental backup plan for everything from a financial crisis to another global pandemic to worse. In the console of my car, I even keep one of those handy-dandy hammers that can shatter your windshield in the event you veer into a river. I mean, you never know.

One of my favorite board games is The Worst-Case Scenario Survival Game. I may not be all that great at Risk or chess, but this is where I shine. Worst-case scenarios are always running through my mind, so I might as well get a board game win out of it. Just another day in the life of an Enneagram 6 spent pondering potential catastrophes. As one does. Creating a busy protocol offers worst-case scenario experts like myself a chance to put all that backup planning to good use.

Remember, the goal when creating a protocol isn't *busy* prevention but *hurry* prevention. We want to show up for our full, rich lives without letting them suffocate us, distract us, or send us scouring the internet for vacant land in the middle of nowhere where we can live completely off the grid. We want to live life to the fullest, not merely survive a life that seems hellbent on taking us down.

When you find yourself on either the precipice of a busy season or drowning in the middle of one, unsure of how exactly you got here, it's time to enact your busy protocol. If stop, drop, and roll are the steps you take if your clothing catches fire, then pause, purge, prune, pass off, and protect are the steps you take when it's your calendar that's on fire. Later in this chapter you're going to actually create your busy protocol. For now, let's take a deeper look at each of these components to better equip you to create your own plan of action.

1. PAUSE

When busyness hits, the very next thing we should do is press pause on adding any new commitments to the calendar for the foreseeable future. Now is *not* the time to offer to bring a dish to the work potluck or volunteer to direct your church's trunk-or-treat festivities. Now is not the time to sign your child up for an extracurricular STEM class or fill your only free evening with social plans. The busy protocol is meant to preserve your remaining capacity. The most vital step in doing that is to avoid taking on more. Instead, it's time to lean hard on your new, go-to line: "I'm so sorry. I don't have the capacity for that right now."

Just last night, my daughter walked into our room at bedtime and spouted off a list of items she needs for school and life. My response was, "You need to make a list. Write it all down. My brain can't hold any more right now." It's far easier to tell that to our kids, though, than it is to tell our churches, schools, colleagues, friends, and extended family. But being willing to speak up is a necessary component to being busy well. Only the tasks, responsibilities, and activities that are both urgent *and* important should take precedence while your busy protocol is in effect.

2. PURGE

The next step in the busy protocol is to move every single thing weighing on you out of your brain and onto a piece of paper. Getting all of those tasks, decisions, appointments, and projects down on paper will offer you a broader look at the many things you're trying to manage so you can then decide how to best handle them going forward.

What is weighing on you now? Do you have any upcoming appointments you're worried you'll forget about? A list of chores lingering in the back of your mind? Have you been putting off important tasks? Are there items you need to grab from the store? What home projects are looming? Which decisions, concerns, or conversations are distracting you from being present? Even the most seemingly insignificant tasks (like replacing burned-out light bulbs) can compound and pull from our capacity.

When we pen our concerns rather than work to juggle them by memory, we turn them into actionable tasks rather than a melody of chaos running through our brains. From here we're able to systematically funnel them through our busy protocol by pausing certain activities, eliminating the inessential, prioritizing the most urgent and important tasks, delegating what we can, and postponing the things that can wait.

3. PRUNE

Once you've stopped adding new capacity-reducing activities and penned your current ones, your next step is to start offloading some of the ones you're already committed to. To make it to the other side of this busy season in one piece, you're going to need to eliminate inessential activities and simplify the essential ones as much as possible.

Eliminate. What can you stop doing? Evaluate your daily routine, to-do list, and commitments to find the things that can immediately get crossed off, at least for the time being. If the only thing you can eliminate for now are your healthy habits, like working out and reading, that's okay. This isn't meant to be a long-term solution. It's a short-term strategy to weather the storm. Just don't forget to resume them once the worst of the storm passes.

Simplify. Yes, your family still needs to eat. However, if your typical MO is an elaborate meal plan and sourdough bread made from scratch, your busy protocol should offer you simpler alternatives. It may involve more takeout or a far simpler go-to meal plan. Perhaps it's time to batch three days' worth of pressure-cooker shredded chicken tacos instead of making hand-stuffed manicotti with homemade spaghetti sauce. Don't worry; your sourdough starter is resilient. It will be just fine until you're able to get back to it.

While your *lengthy* workout routine may be sitting the bench or you're forced to forgo your *weekly* date night for the time being, perhaps there's a way to have your cake and eat it too. Instead of succumbing to atrophy or sacrificing quality time with your spouse altogether, look for the air pockets that can accommodate a modified workout and short but sweet mini-dates. Five minutes of lunges will still get your blood pumping, and a brief walk around the block with your spouse beats no alone time at all.

4. PASS OFF

On a trip to Kauai, Hawaii, my husband and I left our shoes in the car and spent the morning strolling down the picturesque Polihale beach. By the time we turned to head back toward our car, the sun had migrated high into the sky. As we left the shore and headed toward the parking lot, we noticed the sand had become hotter than when we first set off. Unbearably hotter. I'd never felt anything like it. We tried running, thinking the speed would alleviate some of the pain, but no luck. Everything in me wanted to just sit down so my feet would stop hurting, but I knew it would hurt just as badly and only slow me down. I just needed to get my whole body off this sand, and fast. At one point I even tried pausing to dig my feet down into the sand, thinking surely there had to be cooler sand below. Instead, it felt as though I'd stuck them directly into a pizza oven.

We must have looked ridiculous, zig-zagging our way to the parking lot, briefly pausing in the shadow of every weed. Paul, with his longer legs and clearly more calloused feet, made it to our car first, while I found myself stranded in a bush next to the scalding hot parking lot. If the sand was that hot, I could only imagine how painful the blacktop was going to be.

I stood there, considering my next step, resigning at this point to just hold up until the sun sets. Suddenly, a car pulled up next to my little bush home, and the back door swung open.

"The sand is hot, yeah?"

I looked up to see three smiling Danish superheroes offering me a ride to my shoes. I ignored all stranger danger and hopped in. These delightful humans drove me to our car, saving my soles.

Step two in our busy protocol: delegation. Desperate times call for desperate measures. When life gets crazy, it's time to let your community lighten your load whenever you can.

One of the ways you can easily find yourself in over your head is by thinking you have to be the one to do it all. Sure, there are certainly things only you can do. My youngest and I have a secret handshake we do when excited, before bed, or when parting ways. Grandma could learn our handshake for the times I'm out of town, but it wouldn't hold the same sentimental weight as it does when I do it. Some things just can't be passed off.

That said, there are plenty of things we can outsource on an as-needed basis. We've paid our neighbor's son to mow our lawn during soccer season. Instead of running to the store for groceries, we'll order them online and have them delivered. Yes, there is a fee for grocery delivery, and tipping your shopper is a must, but when we're extra busy, it's a lifesaver. It helps me avoid impulse shopping, stick with my simpler meal plan, and relieve my mental load of an errand. Win, win, win. Oh, and one could say it's cheaper than therapy. Another win.

We've carpooled to practices, asked Grandma to chaperone a field trip, and called upon our neighbor to watch one of our kiddos for the evening.

On top of delegating to friends, family, or local resources, we can delegate to those who live within our own homes too. We can redistribute household chores among our kids and swap assumed responsibilities and roles with our partners.

I think it's important to pause here and acknowledge we don't all have the same resource pool from which to pull. Relationship status, family dynamics, finances, and geography all contribute to our ability to lean on others for help when needed. The fact of the matter is some of us are out there putting one foot in front of the other, day after day, without the help we could use. Access to support is a privilege we shouldn't be taking lightly. If you have it, use it with gratitude. If it's not easy to come by for you, you'll need to lean a little harder on the other components of your protocol. You may need to eliminate a little more ruthlessly and simplify further than you would otherwise. Being busy well means we work with what we've got to prioritize the things that matter most.

Keep in mind, too, that sometimes finding community means you've got to be willing to sign yourself up for another commitment. It's a catch-22—a "You gotta spend money to make money" sort of situation. I found one of my dearest friends by joining a stroller boot camp when my oldest was just a baby. Community can be found through book clubs, moms groups, church, places of employment, in the classroom, on the playground, or simply by getting to know people in your very own neighborhood. Investing in community when you're unbusy or less busy can pay dividends later as you navigate busier seasons together.

5. PROTECT

Just as we must prevent the influx of new commitments on the front end, we also want to protect the end of our busy seasons as well. The most important part of initiating a busy protocol, in fact, is identifying when it's going to come to an end. It could be a few days from now or much further into the future.

As I sat in our doctor's office, listening to her explain the importance of reducing physical activity and stimulation while my son recovered from his lingering concussion, I couldn't help but equate it with the principles for surviving a busy season. (That's sort of what happens when you write a book: everything you hear becomes potential book content. If you interact with me while I'm writing a book, you just may land in it.)

What she wanted Jameson to do during the initial post-concussive period was to avoid any activities that would raise his heart rate, increase his blood pressure, or put him at risk of receiving another blow to the head, *which is a nearly impossible task for teenage boys.*

Here's a brief synopsis of how she explained it to him: Your brain is always at work. It keeps your heart pumping, lungs functioning, pain receptors alert, digestive track working, and the oxygen in your blood circulating. It's doing its job whether you're paying attention to it or not. On top of that, you use your brain for plenty of important activities throughout your day: activities such as focusing on school, having a conversation, thinking critically, walking from class to class, maintaining your balance, doing your homework, and making a sandwich. And then, *on top of all that,* you stress it even further by doing physical activities that raise your heart rate and blood pressure. While recovering from a concussion, your brain needs you to eliminate as many inessential activities as possible. This means not piling more onto its already busy workload of keeping you alive by breathing oxygen and pumping blood. If you want your brain to heal fully and efficiently, you must reduce as much of its workload as possible.

During busy seasons, we should be protecting our capacity as if it has received a blow to the head: by offloading tasks and reducing stimulation wherever possible. A busy protocol not only serves as a method for preventing further injury; it also allows us a chance to fully recover.

Find the light at the end of the tunnel and ruthlessly protect it with a hefty layer of bubble wrap. Being present during your busy seasons requires you to ensure there is reprieve on the horizon.

Now, some busy seasons don't have a clear-cut end date. While sports seasons and the holidays tend to have more obvious conclusions, things like relationship issues, illness, injuries, and work crises don't. If it's lingering busyness you're experiencing right now, try looking ahead for a point in time when your load will start to lighten or for a small air pocket in the midst of the chaos. Then protect that space at all costs. When it arrives, you'll be so glad you did.

Say no to upcoming commitments, take a season off, or leave a weekend free to prioritize recreation and connection. Or just hold one evening free of activities if that's all the space you can protect right now.

A MESSAGE FOR THE FAMILY SAFETY NET

I'm the family safety net. My work hours allow me more flexibility than my husband's do, which leaves me volunteering as tribute whenever our plans get hijacked. If a kid spikes a fever, nine times out of ten I'm the one looking for work coverage or rearranging all my plans. I'm not upset about it. In fact, personally, I prefer it this way.

Maybe roles are reversed in your home, or perhaps you and your spouse take turns placing your well-laid plans on the chopping block of parenting. No matter the arrangement, when we're setting goals, cultivating habits, and making plans, we tend to forget what raising kids requires of us.

This is why realistic expectations and seasonal living are so important. There are beneficial principles we can take away from time-management experts. But for those of us who must regularly reconfigure our plans because of parenting or caregiving of any kind, how we implement those principles will vary. "Consistency is the key," they say. Well, tell that to my middle schooler who can't seem to stop breaking fingers in gym class. I can plan out my consistent healthy habits and work schedule, but when I get a call from the school, it all goes out the window—again.

If you tend to function as the safety net in your home, it's important to properly communicate when it's time to enact a busy protocol to those you live with. This way you'll be able to redistribute the weight more quickly and evenly.

YOUR BUSY PROTOCOL

It's time to craft your own busy protocol. You'll find a template on page 183. You can write there, directly inside the book, make a copy, or grab a sheet of paper and rewrite the outline. You may want to refer to the brain dump you made in chapter 5 or create a new one.

As a reference, here is an example of my own personal busy protocol:

Busy Protocol

1 **Pause**
Stop creating social media content, decline new social plans for myself and my kids, let the house go for now, leave the extended family text thread unread.

2 **Purge**
Brain dump every single task, to-do, project, errand, item to purchase, decision, etc. that is weighing on you. Leave the paper out and add to it whenever something else comes to mind.

3 **Prune**
Evaluate your current commitments and responsibilities. Identify the ones you can ruthlessly eliminate or simplify.

Example:

Simplify/Eliminate/Postpone

Short, at-home workout

Pause creating social media content

Reschedule dinner with friends

Simpler meal plan

4 **Pass Off**

Grandma to pick up kids

Paul to call the plumber

Takeout dinner on game days

Schedule grocery delivery

5 **Protect**

No spring sports this year. Keep Sundays free of plans. Bubble wrap the weekend after soccer season ends.

Look at a busy protocol like a contingency plan to empower you. Rather than getting tossed around, relying on balance and happenstance to maneuver your way through chaotic seasons, you've got an actionable plan that works. Something that lets you take back the reins and make decisions related to your time, energy, and attention with greater intention.

You may discover that you don't actually have a time-management problem at all. You may, in fact, figure out that you *can* tackle this season effectively with the twenty-four hours each day we're all allotted.

TIP FOR BEING BUSY WELL: PRIORITIZE LIKE THERE'S A POWER OUTAGE

Did you know *priorities* wasn't ever pluralized until the 1900s? Prior to then, the word was just *priority*: as in one, singular, most important thing. Now, we've all got a list of them.

Still, you can decide which things to prioritize by viewing your calendar like it's a home experiencing a power outage. Let's say you've got a generator, but it's only strong enough to run the essentials. What do you power? Probably your refrigerator, to preserve the food. Depending on the time of year, you may need to run your furnace for warmth and to keep the pipes from freezing. You probably won't be running power to your washing machine or dishwasher, as those tasks can wait.

While functioning in your busy protocol, you are going to be shifting your capacity to only the most essential tasks. After that, you want to focus any and all remaining margin on activities that can help restore your capacity. That may include connecting with your kids, reading a book, taking a walk, or resetting your kitchen before bed so the morning can run more smoothly.

CHAPTER NINE

Be Prepared

The Importance of Creating a Busy Protocol

The first time my son had a middle-of-the-night asthma attack, I just about lost it. Yes, I'm a nurse, and nurses are not supposed to lose it. I've assisted in resolving some of the most emergent of emergencies throughout my nursing career. There were plenty of times I felt rattled, but my patients would have never known. Remaining calm, cool, and collected was my actual job.

But when it comes to my kids, I am anything but calm, cool, and collected. That night, I'd be willing to bet even the neighbors across the street could hear my heart pounding. Being shaken awake at two in the morning by your wheezing four-year-old ages you. I remember shouting instructions at my husband and frantically searching for pants while calling 911. It was sheer and utter panic.

It's been quite a few years since that eventful night, and we've handled a few more asthma attacks since then. Each time I was a little calmer and more collected than the last. With experience comes competence and confidence. In fact, I can now spot the signs of an impending asthma attack well before it becomes an actual emergency. I don't have to wait until I'm being shaken awake in the middle of the night to know there's a problem. I've learned to spot the red flags hours in advance. You can hear it in the cough, or by the atypical increase in respiration rate after mild exertion. Now I'll simply pause while loading the dishwasher to give my son the side eye. "Do you think you need your inhaler?"

SIX SIGNS HURRY IS ON THE HORIZON

We don't have to wait until we're in over our heads to implement a busy protocol. Instead, we can learn to spot the warning signs ahead of time before they develop into a crisis. Instead of waiting until our frantic, unsustainable pace catches up to us, we can learn to spot hurry coming a mile away and prepare accordingly. Let's take a look at six red flags that would indicate a busy protocol is in order.

1. Your Calendar Is Getting Hijacked

Just because your calendar is full doesn't mean you're destined for hurry. When we put time, effort, and intentionality into our calendars, we can strategically fill them in a way that leaves us enough breathing room to accommodate a bit of chaos. When we know we're going to be busy, we can plan accordingly.

Yet one of the first signs hurry is on the horizon is when you find your calendar getting hijacked by unforeseen circumstances. This is when things start to get dicey. When we're forced to squeeze in last-minute appointments, sacrifice our working hours, rearrange our day, or give up our much-needed margin, it sets the stage for hurried living. It can happen quickly and when we least expect it.

Like helpless bystanders, we witness time and time again as the margin we intentionally left ourselves gets eaten up by circumstances outside our control. When unexpected errands, appointments, and emergencies start encroaching on your calendar, hurry is likely to follow. When you start to see it happening, it's time to downshift into your busy protocol.

2. You Avoid People and Responsibilities

One of the most ominous signs of hurried living is when we find ourselves dodging human interaction and responsibilities. Instead of responding to texts, we ghost our friends. Instead of making appointments, we put them off. A five-minute phone call to simply order more contact lenses feels as burdensome as a trip to the DMV. The next thing you know, you're digging through your travel backpack in search of extra contacts because you're now desperately low.

I've found it helpful to warn close friends of my tendency to go AWOL. This way, instead of being offended when I ghost them, they can swoop in to help. My friend Becky has been known to text me something to the effect of, "Are you hanging in there okay? You've not responded to my texts, so I assume you're drowning. Do you need anything?"

Perhaps the best thing you can do for yourself is to find a friend who doesn't get offended by your wild fluctuations in capacity. If you notice yourself ghosting friends and procrastinating typically easy tasks, it's probably time to initiate your busy protocol.

3. You Feel Increasingly Irritable

Different things can cause you to grow irritable—your kids washing their hands in your homemade chicken broth, for example. But when you're hurried, irritability is guaranteed. I'll start snapping at my kids over relatively minor infractions, like leaving their shoes sprawled all over the house. *I mean, for the love of all that is good, just put your shoes away.* But this isn't something that usually sends me into a total tailspin. Not unless my capacity is hanging on by a thread.

When we're already living at a frenetic pace, it doesn't take much to push us over the edge. Pay attention when you feel increased irritability, because it is a sign that it's time to delegate, eliminate something, or prioritize a nice long walk in the woods.

4. You Drop the Ball

I can't juggle. Literally, I can't juggle two tennis balls. When I try to manage too many activities at once, I start dropping those as well. Did you know our brains are really only capable of holding onto four things at once? Researchers at the University of Oregon have found that "the human brain has a built-in limit on the number of discrete thoughts it can entertain at one time. The limit for most individuals is four." This is why purging is such an important component to the busy protocol. It helps us see all we're trying to manage at once—which is clearly more than four things.

Wouldn't it be nice if we only had four things to manage at the same time? While science tells us our capacity is limited, society continues to prod us beyond our limits. We expect ourselves to be able to juggle more than we should, and then we kick ourselves for falling apart. It reminds me of the time I stopped into the kindergarten class to check on a student. There were a few students trying to give the teacher their work at the same time, and chaos was slowing beginning to erupt. That's when Mrs. Person said to them, "Please sit back down. One at a time. I'm not an octopus."

Instead of trying to grow extra arms to assist you in carrying even more, consider dropping the ball as your brain waving a white flag in surrender. Missed appointments and forgotten field trips are just another way your body is telling you you've taken on too much.

My daughter hates cleaning her bedroom. "I can't," she tells me, "It's too much!" This is when I like to remind her that if it feels like too much to tackle, maybe it's because it is, literally, too much. The more stuff you have, the more work it takes to tidy it. In many cases, that same minimalist principle can be applied to our time. It's not always true of every situation, but it *is* important to consider whether you're struggling to get it all done simply because you're trying to do too much. Plain and simple.

5. You Are Distracted

"Mom, you're like a poor Wi-Fi connection." Those were the words of my then-eleven-year-old as she tried to tell me a story while I was giving her my very, very divided attention. When I'm functioning in a state of hurry—trying to have a conversation, make dinner, and figure out exactly where tonight's basketball game is located while also responding to a work email—I start buffering.

While moving through a task list a mile long, our brains can't focus on the present moment and the people directly in front of us. If you find yourself spending more time distracted than you are present, there's a good chance you're living hurriedly.

Multitasking is just as much an archaic approach to time management as the food pyramid from the 1990s is to good nutrition. While that food pyramid made us feel good about eating our highly processed, fat-free foods back then, it turns out it wasn't all that nutritious. Today we know more about nutrition, and we know more about managing our time well, too. Multitasking came on the scene in the 1960s and was used to describe an IBM system's capabilities. Eventually, someone decided to apply the concept to our human capabilities, and we started believing the narrative that humans could multitask as well. We bought into the idea that by dividing our attention and doing multiple things at once, we could get more done.

Yet multitasking only left us with the illusion of productivity. While we thought we were managing our time well, we were merely distributing tiny shards of our attention among the things that matter instead of actually giving those things the attention they deserve.

6. You Are Unavailable

If you flat out don't have time to make it to your grandkid's sporting events, play a round of Uno with your daughter before dinner, or do any of the things that fill you up, you might be approaching margin-deprivation levels of hurry.

Pay attention to how you're responding to the things you typically love to do: "I didn't get out fishing much this summer." "I don't remember the last time we had a date night." "I just don't have the time to go hunting this year." "I'll try and make it to the last half of the game, but it's going to be tight." "I will snuggle with you tomorrow night. Right now, Mama is about to fall asleep standing up."

Becoming unavailable for the things that matter most to you can occur within a busy season. It happens. But it can also be the result of giving your attention to the wrong sort of things. Regardless of what is causing your lack of availability, when you find it happening, it's time to initiate your busy protocol.

SYMPTOM MANAGEMENT ISN'T A LONG-TERM SOLUTION

Let's say you cut your hand. You'd be able to tell if it was becoming infected by the symptoms it exhibits. Infection at the site can cause redness, swelling, warmth, bleeding, and pain. You could work to treat each of those symptoms individually by taking pain medication, applying ice, or wrapping it with a pressure bandage. But none of those actions will resolve the ongoing infection. If you treat the source of the infection, the symptoms will take care of themselves.

When overwhelmed, we often go into survival mode and start managing the symptoms of hurry while the root cause runs rampant. We might address the fact that we keep dropping the ball by purchasing a better planner, setting more alerts on our phone, or using our limited margin to accomplish more tasks. We notice we're missing out on the things that matter, so we willingly spread ourselves thinner and thinner to squeeze it all in.

Or, after a day of feeling overly distracted, we resort to guilt and shame for having missed out on the important matters. Instead of addressing why we were so easily distracted, we spiral into shame and self-pity.

When all signs point to hurry, the way out isn't doubling down on symptom management but rather replenishing your capacity. In time, instead of panicking when things start to go south, you'll respond with confidence, having already spotted the signs of hurry coming a mile away. The more you practice a strategic approach to busyness, the better equipped you'll become at spotting those warning signs of hurry in advance and then resolving them before they overwhelm you.

WHEN TO INITIATE YOUR BUSY PROTOCOL

The thing to remember about your busy protocol is that it's not meant to remain in place indefinitely. If every time a pilot flew an aircraft they found themselves enacting emergency protocols, they wouldn't be a pilot for long.

While some busy seasons will last longer than others, the goal is to make sure those busy seasons don't become a way of life. If you're living every season at max capacity, it may be the result of your overcommitment, unwillingness to say no, and inability to protect your margin year-round. If that's you, then perhaps it's because you're more comfortable with the chaos than you are with a calmer way of life.

That's how I lived for years: overly busy and overly cluttered. It wasn't until I became overly over it that I was able to finally see what was really at play. I hid behind the chaos, using hurry as a negative coping strategy to avoid working on the areas of my life in need of growth. I didn't mean to. It's just what I did. In fact, even now it tends to be my go-to. I've still got a few more chapters to lay down in this book, and every fiber of my being feels like running some errands to avoid sitting here. This is hard work. I mean, I'm not building a bridge with my bare hands or anything, but writing a whole book that makes some semblance of sense is mentally strenuous and ridiculously time-consuming. It's tempting to fill my calendar with impulse shopping, busywork, and nonurgent errands so that I can avoid clickity-clacking away as my coffee gets cold.

The difference now is that I know what's up. I'm on to myself. I'm aware of my tendency to stick my head in the sand and clutter up my calendar as a means of escape. So I shake my head and press on toward the finish line as my deadline nears.

Your busy protocol is a tool to help you navigate the treacherous waters of a chaotic calendar before resuming a more sustainable pace when they calm back down. Sometimes we have the luxury of predicting busier seasons, and other times, we're inundated out of nowhere. There are two ways we can initiate a busy protocol. One is to plan for it. And the second is to pivot into it.

Plan for It

For accountants, tax season is a predictably busy time of year, right? Retail store owners prepare for the busy holiday shopping season, and landscape companies know their phones will start to blow up once the snow melts and trees begin to bud. If you take a step back and look at your calendar through a wide-angle lens, I bet you can pinpoint typically busier seasons in your life as well.

Take the month of May, which is absolute May-*hem* for parents of school-aged children. The same goes for back-to-school season. With all three of my kids playing fall soccer, late August to early November is a particularly busy season around here. When we know a busy season is coming down the pipeline, we can initiate our protocols ahead of time. We can preemptively simplify our meal plans, set up carpools, clear the clutter, cull our wardrobes, forgo making plans, and redistribute the responsibilities within our home. It's go time.

Pivot into It

Not every season of chaos, however, can be planned for. Perhaps you're dealing with an unprecedented situation at work that has you working late for the next few weeks. Maybe the flu made its way into your home, and everyone is dropping like flies. Perhaps a close friend is experiencing a personal crisis, and she has you on call to help. Or maybe your son was thrown to the ground during gym class, and all the preemptive prep work you did for your busy season just isn't enough.

You don't need me to tell you that life is unpredictable. You've experienced it before, and you will again. We don't have to move through life glumly longing to survive seasons of busyness when they arise. In the words of Eleanor Roosevelt, "It takes as much energy to wish as it does to plan." Winging it isn't an effective or sustainable survival strategy. Instead, we can proactively create an effective emergency plan to help us arrive safely at our next destination, on the other side of the chaos.

The thing most responsible for stealing our time isn't soccer season, end-of-school festivities, work emergencies, or even unforeseen injuries. You could say that it's actually depleted by our excessive generosity—not our generosity toward others, though, but our generous donation of time and attention to the handheld computers we tote around in our back pockets all day. Our phones just may be robbing us of even more time and attention than our excessive busyness does.

TIP FOR BEING BUSY WELL: HARNESS THE POWER OF RELENTLESS FOCUS

In our home, I'm notorious for simultaneously making dinner, writing a new article, and replying to texts—all while the laundry is half folded, the groceries only half put away, and the other article I *was* working on left halfway done. I refer to them as *halfway days*, and they usually occur when I'm overwhelmed and feeling hurried. It's next to impossible to be fully present while leapfrogging from one half-finished project to the next.

I once asked my husband how he manages to clean the kitchen so quickly and efficiently. His answer was simple, yet profound: "Relentless focus. I start at one side, and swoop across the kitchen, never moving on before tidying the space directly in front of me." It seems so simple, yet if you've gotten in the habit of halfway living, it's surprisingly difficult.

Instead of letting tasks linger, tackle them immediately by intentionally tapping into a bit of relentless focus. For some, staying on task and focused comes easy. For others (ahem, me), it takes effort and intentionality. Depending on the task, sometimes I even have to say it out loud: "Okay, relentless focus, Rachelle. Relentless focus." When we cross tasks off our to-do list early on, we prevent them from becoming urgent matters later. Make the appointment now, take the trash all the way to the curb, empty the sink of *all* dirty dishes instead of a few at a time. By being hyper-proactive and relentlessly focused, we can keep our mental loads lighter and keep margin deprivation at bay.

CHAPTER TEN

Be Unreachable

The Importance of Eliminating Digital Distractions

Has a seemingly insignificant encounter, haphazard comment, or random thought changed the way you view something, forever? There you are, minding your own business, living your life, when you're abruptly thrust into a new reality.

That's how change seems to happen for me. I need to be shaken awake by some kind of rock-bottom moment. I mean, not the rockiest of bottoms. It's not like I've ever gambled away our home or embezzled money. My rock-bottom moments tend to be more melodramatic than anything. Still, they are significant enough to force a permanent change in thinking. They shift something inside of me, changing much more than just my daily routine. They go deep, recalibrating a little slice of my identity along the way, leaving me living a little more in line with what I value most in this world. It was exactly that kind of unexpected encounter that led me to minimalism—and it's exactly how I started being more present and available for, in the words of poet Mary Oliver, my "one wild and precious life."

It was a Saturday morning—or perhaps a Friday evening. The details are a bit of a blur, and they don't really matter anyway. All

I remember is that my entire family was downstairs hanging out while I was sitting on my bed, scrolling through Instagram.

I hadn't gone upstairs to hide from my family and consume some social media content. That's rarely how it happens, though, is it? No, I went upstairs to spend some time doing what I loosely refer to as "work," which means creating an Instagram post and responding to comments and direct messages. It's easy to forget that work didn't always involve social media. Back in the day, we all just did our jobs. Teachers taught, nurses saved the world, parents parented, realtors helped people buy and sell homes, and on and on. We all just went to work and—well, worked.

The same went for writing and publishing books. You would write the book, speak at a few bookstores, and maybe go on a book tour if you happened to be a big deal. That was that. Your publisher carried most of the marketing load, while you focused on crafting a book people would want to read. Today, however, whether you want to sell books, real estate, or handmade earrings, you *also* need to be an online content creator. Sigh.

When I finally finished "working" that day, I didn't immediately head back downstairs to reengage with my family as I had intended. Instead, at some point, I went from creating content to consuming it. There I sat, for who knows how long, scrolling through Instagram Reels and sharing the best ones with my sisters. *Obviously.* Eventually I came across a video I'll never forget. This one would change everything.

No, it wasn't a beautiful photo montage reminding me of the good ole days. It wasn't even an inspiring quote about putting down our phones to pick up our lives. I've seen those dozens of times. Heck, I've even created those posts.

No, this time I found myself watching someone brush their arm hair with what appeared to be—a toothbrush? I can still picture it.

I tossed down my phone. That was it. The algorithm had gone too far, and I wanted out. It was as if I'd gotten a glimpse of a glitch in the matrix. What was I *doing*? Why was I giving this precious time away to someone's arm hair? This was my opportunity for rest, connection, and play. Instead of banking some capacity, I was sliding further into debt. I was draining my limited mental energy and time on the pointless consumption of digital content.

Perhaps if this had been the first time I'd found myself hypnotized by social media, it wouldn't have had such an impact. But it wasn't. While I may not have happened upon this kind of weirdly disturbing arm hair content before, I can't even begin to tell you the number of times I inadvertently donated my time and attention to big tech. This was Instagram's Icarus moment for me. It flew just too close to the sun, and I was done. In that moment, I knew that *this* was not how I'd be spending another moment of my time.

THE STATS DON'T LIE

We're all quick to agree that time spent on social media doesn't hold a candle to quality time spent investing in the things that deeply matter to us. Spending time with family and friends or on hobbies, unique experiences, and meaningful work wins out every time. If asked in advance, nobody would intentionally choose to watch random arm hair content over, say, eating waffles with their kids. Yet the way in which we just give away the very thing we claim not to have enough of? Well, it would indicate otherwise.

Have you ever looked at your screen-time stats? Take a moment to peruse the settings on your phone and find your screen time. Take it a step further and look at your pick-ups. In the settings, you can literally see the number of times you look at your phone every day. When I first did this, it was alarming. I had no idea how many times a day I was absentmindedly reaching for my phone.

If I were to tell you about a friend of mine who continually sucked the life out of me, you'd recommend I set up better boundaries with that friend. Maybe you'd even suggest I eliminate this friend from my life altogether. Wouldn't you? Or if I were seeking advice about a friend who left me feeling bad about myself or comparing myself to others, you'd likely suggest I take a break from this friend.

Your phone is not a good friend. Sure, it swoops in to save the day from time to time, occasionally offering directions, entertainment, or inspiring words of wisdom. But much of the time it leaves us feeling a little emptier than when we first picked it up.

Don't get me wrong. I love the fact that my online work lets me have conversations with like-hearted people all over the world. I've given and received advice to and from people from Australia to Canada, and from France to Puerto Rico.

That said, the phone can't (and shouldn't) replace the people directly in front of us. An hour of sharing Instagram reels with my sisters simply can't do to my soul what an hour of laughing with them over a bowl of cookie dough can. Twenty minutes of mushroom hunting in the woods fills my soul in a way that twenty minutes of online shopping never could. Yet time and time again, we head into the digital matrix to numb out in the name of relaxation.

Why? Well, for a few reasons. One, it has become a habit. The average American picks up their phone 144 times a day. Imagine if you habitually hugged your kids, did a push-up, tidied a corner of your home, or wrote a sentence in the book you've been meaning to write at that same rate. You'd get so much done.

It's not that our actual priorities are out of whack. We're well aware that screen time isn't the best use of our attention. Yet we let ourselves fall victim to arm-hair-combing videos while true productivity, connection, rest, and play fall by the wayside. The siren song of dopamine is loud and relentless, friend, and our phones offer a quick hit. It's far easier to get a dopamine boost by checking for likes, scrolling for news updates, or sending funny content online than by partaking in more meaningful activities. Our phones are sitting at our fingertips while the more meaningful activities often take a bit of energy and forethought.

We have to plan ahead to hunt for mushrooms or spend time with a friend. Going for a walk during the winter takes properly layering up. Writing a book, or any truly meaningful work, takes a significant degree of vulnerability and authenticity. Our phones, though? They are just sitting there next to us, waiting to be unlocked.

THIS IS YOUR BRAIN ON TECH

If you're a parent (or really if you have just been in close proximity to a child), odds are good you've witnessed the effects too much screen time has on kids. Perhaps you allowed them a little bit of "tech time," as we refer to it in our home, and the next thing you know, far too much time has passed. As they say, time flies when you're having fun, whether it's fake or real fun. Maybe they were up at the crack of dawn and you need to buy yourself some silence while drinking your coffee. Perhaps you scheduled back-to-back video calls for work, forgetting they don't have school today. Netflix can be a heck of a babysitter in a bind. Or maybe you got caught up talking with your sister on the phone, and the one twenty-three-minute episode you intended for them to watch turned into three of them. *Oops.* Whether on purpose or by accident, at some point we've all allowed our kids more screen time than we intended to.

As a result, we have watched as they morph into some weird version of themselves. In my experience, too much tech time tends to turn a kid into either a forceful dictator or incapacitated sloth. They either start making demands like they own the place, or they become incapable of contributing anything to our home for the foreseeable future. I'll find them just lying on the ground, on the stairs, or on the couch as if they've completely forgotten how to use their limbs. There's rarely an in-between.

It's not their fault. My brain does the same thing. Any time I spend too much time consuming technology, I feel the same way. I walk away somehow feeling both overstimulated and overly tired at the very same time. On top of that, I'm left with this nagging feeling of regret, knowing I just wasted more of my life watching other people live theirs.

It's not just that we're terrible at managing our time; we're fighting an uphill battle against what is called "dopaminergic excitement." Or rather, a battle against "the thrill of anticipation." The urge to check our phones for no good reason is a habit we've developed thanks to our brain chemicals. Dopamine isn't released in response to pleasure; it's released in *anticipation* of pleasure. You don't have to actually enjoy the results to get a hit of dopamine. Dopamine is the reason we start planning our next vacation before we're even home from the last one. It's why slot machines are hard for many people to walk away from. And it's the reason we keep scrolling through social media when we don't even enjoy the content. You don't even care about the pictures of your coworker's cat or an influencer's morning skin care routine. Yet you keep on scrolling, because dopamine is one heck of a drug. It's not the content we're addicted to; it's the anticipation of what may pop up next.

As Oliver Burkeman puts it in *Four Thousand Weeks*,

> The contemporary online "attention economy," of which we've heard so much in recent years: it's essentially a giant machine for persuading you to make the wrong choices about what to do with your attention, and therefore with your finite life, by getting you to care about things you didn't want to care about. And you have far too little control over your attention simply to decide, as if by fiat, that you're not going to succumb to its temptations.

Companies that profit from our screen-time usage don't want us to reduce our use of technology in this way. They simply can't afford for us to live a more present and engaged life. They count on our inability to resist scrolling for dopamine in hopes of selling us something in the process. In his book *Digital Minimalism*, Cal Newport writes,

> Many attention economy companies want you to think about their services in a binary way: either you use it, or you don't. This allows them to entice you into their ecosystem with some feature you find important, and then, once you're a "user," deploy attention engineering to overwhelm you with integrated options, trying to keep you engaging with their service well beyond your original purpose.

The phone is designed to get you relying on it for something important so that it can grab hold of your attention in a million other little ways. Basically, when we're off our phones, tech companies and advertisers can't tell us which décor trends are moving out of style, which boots we must have *this* fall, or which kitchen gadget is saving some influencer's life right now. Best business practices are the ones that keep customers logged in, and therefore subconsciously shopping, as much as possible.

Sometimes we claim to be short on time, but based on how often we're picking up our phones, it's safe to say it isn't as much a time issue as it is a matter of attention. In my experience, the easiest way to escape our compulsive consumption is a forced hiatus.

ACCIDENTAL PHONE FAST

My son is an avid fisherman. He's been fishing with his grandpa since preschool. This summer, he saved up enough of his own hard-earned money to buy a small flat-bottom fishing boat with a 4-horsepower 1980 Evinrude motor. She's a beauty. What better way to escape your sisters and their friends than puttering on out into the middle of the lake for some solo fishing time?

During his maiden voyage, I had my phone in one hand, ready to capture a photo, while using the other to help untie the back of his boat. Suddenly, inexplicably, and almost ceremoniously, my phone slipped out of my hand and sank to the bottom of the lake. I could see it down on the lake floor, camera open and ready to capture the moment. So close, yet so far away.

The odd thing was, as a person whose life motto is more like "panic first, think later," I felt an eerie calm. It was as if, deep down, I sort of *wanted* it to be broken. Not because I was eager for a new phone, but because I wanted no phone. In a world of increasing connectivity, I was at a point where I found myself craving less of it. Instead of fearing the water damage, I was secretly hoping for it.

My nephew hopped off the dock and retrieved my phone within a matter of seconds, but it was DOA. Because it was a long holiday weekend, I spent the next few days without a phone altogether. Once it was replaced, I then spent another week waiting to gain access to my iCloud and social accounts, because of course I couldn't remember any of my passwords.

This phone-free week was probably the most grounded and engaged I'd been in a long time. Without access to my contacts, email, and social accounts, I found being present in the moment to be a piece of cake. I felt more clear headed and somehow both more rested and more productive. While I grew up with pay phones, paper maps, and patiently waiting *weeks* for catalog orders to arrive in the mail, most of my adult life has been characterized by easy access to this pocket-sized dopamine slot machine.

At first glance, the answer seems simple: ditch the smartphone. Yet that isn't necessarily a viable option. I've also read dozens of books and articles offering practical solutions to reducing screen time. The strategies include things like: buy a flip phone instead, delete all your social apps, initiate a smartphone sabbath once a week, and even seal your phone in a safe for the weekend.

While these strategies hold merit, they only work when we use them. And in my experience, we can't always use them. But we will get to that in a minute. So what's the solution? Where does this leave us? If we can't ditch our smartphones, are we left to simply succumb to them? Not at all. Instead, we can create sustainable phone habits that will help us inch toward our goal of living more present and attentive lives.

REDUCE DIGITAL DISTRACTIONS

In my experience, practical solutions to any problem are best implemented when they are accompanied by a new way of thinking as well. It's far harder to change our habits when we don't have a solid motivation behind them. To use our phones with more intention and better boundaries, we must first address our mindset surrounding our use of technology. Here are three mindset shifts that can help take back our time from the grips of screen time.

1. Implement the Gummy Bear Principle

Gummy bears are my go-to road-trip snack. Well, gummy bears and Cheez-Its. (I know. The picture of nutrition. I'm a nurse, not a registered dietician.) The best thing I can do for myself on a road trip is just not buy them at all. But I do. Every time. And when there's a bag of gummy bears sitting on my console, I don't stand a chance. I'll just chomp away for miles before realizing I've eaten almost the whole bag. The only way to stop devouring them while driving is to chuck them out of reach to the back of my car. Otherwise, I'll consume every single delicious gummy.

When it comes to resisting the things that lure us in, proximity is everything. The gummy bear principle says this: if you were trying to eat less processed sugar, you wouldn't carry a bag of gummy bears around in your back pocket all day. Why, then, do we carry our phone around with us all day and expect to resist reaching for it? Creating distance between you and your phone is the best way to ensure you stay off it. Breaking any kind of addiction is easier when you don't have to stare it down every day.

"In 2014, the U.S. Surgeon General concluded that smoke-free laws in workplaces and communities help smokers quit and reduce tobacco use." When employers created smoke-free work environments, cessation rates among employees improved and smoking prevalence dropped. Employees who couldn't smoke at work were less likely to continue smoking altogether. We can take that same approach to our screen time. You'll end up on your phone less often if it's not charging on your nightstand or traveling around in your back pocket with you all day.

One popular strategy for reducing screen time is to create "office hours" for your phone. This involves refusing to check your emails, messages, voicemails, or texts until a predetermined time each day. During this window of time, you're free to read emails, make calls, and respond to messages. But when the window closes, so does your phone. It's meant to help limit your distractable hours. While, in theory, it's a great idea and may be easily implemented at work, with an administrative assistant to field emergencies for you, it doesn't tend to work for everyday life.

As a school nurse, my job description literally requires me to interrupt a parent's workday. So I know full well that disconnecting from your phone for extended periods of time isn't always an option. Parents who miss my call tend to call back in a bit of a panic: "I'm so sorry I missed your call. Is everything all right?" A febrile, puking, or concussed child doesn't care when your phone's "office hours" are. They just want you to come get them.

What works better during certain seasons in our lives is to allot *out*-of-office hours. It's quite similar, but the expectation is wildly different. When creating out-of-office hours, we are setting more realistic time frames for our unavailability.

Currently, my out-of-office hours include the first one to two hours of my day and the last two to three. What does this look like? Well, when I wake up in the morning, my phone stays asleep. I get up, drink coffee, maybe write some words, work out, wake my kids for school, and help pack lunches—all before even checking my phone. (For the record, this did backfire once when I completely missed the snow day message from our school. So maybe if you notice some snow, give it a quick glance.) Then, at the end of the day, around roughly 8 p.m. or so, I put my phone to bed for the night and don't look at it again until the next day. If you text me at 9 p.m., I'm most likely not getting the message until the next morning—after I've had my coffee.

It's a simple solution I once believed to be impossible because my phone was my alarm clock. Just because your phone *can* double as an alarm clock doesn't mean it has to. For less than $20, you can buy an actual alarm clock, and in so doing, give yourself some much-needed distance from your phone. Yes, this minimalist is recommending you purchase something. That's how beneficial it has been for me.

Buying an alarm clock has single-handedly had the biggest impact on improving my sleep and reducing my daily screen time. Instead of sleeping with your phone within arm's reach, plug it in far away from you. You'll know where it is in an emergency, but you're not likely to get out of your warm bed to check it without a darn good reason.

Of course, I'm going to encourage you to pause here and first recall the season of life you're in. You may currently *have* to have that phone next to your bed, ringer at full volume, as you await the arrival of your first grandbaby. Maybe you're on call at night for work, have a new driver in the family, or a child with a health condition that requires your immediate availability. Plugging in your phone and walking away just isn't always an option.

You're going to have to set realistic screen-free expectations, and then you're going to have to intentionally carve out even smaller chunks of out-of-office hours that work for your current situation. Consider using the settings on your phone to silence specific text message strings that easily draw you in. Keep the important and urgent alerts turned on, and then hush all nonurgent and unimportant notifications.

2. Do More Things That Make You Forget to Check Your Phone

The best days in life are usually the ones when we're too present to even think about checking our phones. I'm talking about the days spent doing something we love so much that we've got all the dopamine and endorphins our bodies need.

For me, it's the days spent baking Lebanese Easter cookies with my kids. Or the summer mornings spent over a bluegill honey hole, catching dozens of keepers. It's taking a family hike through Algonquin Provincial Park hoping for a moose sighting, or scouring Englewood Beach, Florida, for hours, looking for shark teeth. It's tubing kids behind the boat, making homemade pizzas at my brother's, or hitting the slopes with my kids. It's evenings playing euchre with friends and mornings spent thrifting with my daughter.

Of course, every moment of every day can't be spent this way. We can, however, use such moments as a blueprint to create simple hobbies, habits, routines, and daily rituals we can look forward to in the same way. Even just one or two hours a week carved out for those smaller, soul-filling, and attention-grabbing activities will add up and have a lasting impact.

In time, imagine how many collective hours you'll have devoted to the people you love and the hobbies that light you up. Doing more things that make you forget to check your phone will only leave you more present and less digitally distracted.

3. Let the People Directly in Front of You Trump Your Phone

This can be an easy one to forget because life is demanding and those demands often come at us through this pocket-sized device. But unless you're waiting for the appliance delivery driver to call with an arrival time or the pediatrician to ring you back, the people in front of you should never take a back seat to whoever is on the other side of that screen.

Our goal should always be to give our attention to what's happening within arm's reach over what's happening on the other side of our phones. That may be inconvenient at times. But addressing the here and now must take precedence, because in this life, it is all we are guaranteed.

It can be difficult, especially when grabbing our phone has become second nature. But it's worth the fight. The key, writes Catherine Price in *How to Break Up with Your Phone*, "is to keep asking yourself the same question, again and again and again: this is your life—what do you want to pay attention to?"

When we look back over history and the problems humanity has had to face, the battle to reclaim the very attention we freely handed over to the digital age seems insignificant. Humanity has had to battle actual threats on every front. Here, our generation is fighting for our *own* attention, from the comfort of our couches. And we're *losing*.

It's not going to get any easier. These phones aren't going anywhere any time soon. Instead of dropping them into a lake or eagerly waiting for the next local wireless outage, we must start asking ourselves that question, again and again and again. What do we want to pay attention to?

TIP FOR BEING BUSY WELL: HIDE AND DON'T SEEK

If you're struggling to steer clear of your phone as the text messages roll in and your dopamine levels drop, ask your partner, child, roommate, or friend to hide it from you. Or consider swapping phones with them.

When my husband and I are out on a date, we'll often swap phones. That way there is little temptation to check in with the outside world, but we're still reachable in an emergency. You can do this at home as well. I hand my phone off to Paul all the time. He's basically my administrative assistant on the weekends.

Who might you entrust your phone to for a period of time? Just be sure they have a good memory. And maybe don't give it to your toddler lest you find it in the toilet.

CHAPTER ELEVEN

Be Uncluttered

The Practice of Owning Less Stuff

Trigger warning: yellowjackets.

I once shared a picture on Instagram of me holding a small garter snake I had caught with my bare hands for my kids to see. People were outraged. The number of messages I received in which people yelled at me for not first providing them with a snake trigger warning blew me away. Apparently not everybody is cool with spontaneous snake photos. So here lies notice well in advance, just in case violent, stinging yellowjackets happen to have a similar effect on you.

I arrived back home from our cottage at the end of the summer and found one lonely little dead yellowjacket on our living room floor. *Eek.* I quickly scooped it up with a piece of paper and tossed it out the door without thinking much of it. Later that evening I found a *live* yellowjacket dancing around my living room window.

Hmm . . . odd, I thought, before quickly and confidently smacking it with the bottom of my Birkenstock. We don't handle bee, wasp, or yellowjacket encounters around here well. While nobody in our home is technically allergic to them, we are all very averse to being stung. I once witnessed my husband hop a deck rail to avoid a bee encounter. Needless to say, I didn't want my kids knowing what I'd found.

But the next day I found two more. That's when I realized something was up. Turns out that when you leave your home unattended for a couple months, these angry little insects can invoke squatter's rights. I immediately called an exterminator, who came out the very next morning, found the hive under a section of siding, and took care of it.

Or so we thought.

Later that afternoon, I heard a loud buzzing noise coming from our living room. At first I ignored it, assuming it was the dryer or the fridge or that maybe our neighbor was weed whacking. For some reason, more yellowjackets never crossed my mind.

When I finally wandered into the living room, I gasped. Dozens of woozy, irritated, displaced yellowjackets were swarming around the window, as more were creeping in through the light fixture on the ceiling. I about died.

The "exterminator" had screwed up. While he intended to eradicate the hive from outside of our home, he only sealed off their exit, forcing them further *into* it. I, of course, immediately called him back, and he assured me they'd be dead by morning. They were not. It quickly became evident that this guy was in over his head. I called another local exterminator, who blatantly refused to come help. Since it was treated poorly the first time, he didn't want to be associated with the job and told me, "I have a reputation to uphold." I kid you not.

In the meantime, we taped off the light fixtures with cardboard and packing tape and covered up the floor vents with heavy boxes. In hindsight, we probably should have just headed to a hotel for the night. Despite our best efforts, Raegan, who was ten at the time, was awakened at three in the morning after being stung in the neck while sleeping. At this point, burning down the house felt like our only viable option.

The clutter in our homes can initially feel like finding a couple of random dead yellowjackets on the floor: disturbing but merely the price of homeownership. If you're going to have a home, now and then a pest is bound to breach it. The same goes for clutter: sometimes an area of your home will be inexplicably inundated with stuff. It's just how it goes, right?

But cluttered corners can also be an indication that something bigger is brewing beneath the surface. In fact, if I could only share one time-management tip with you it would be this: *drastically* reduce the material possessions within your home. Don't just declutter; de-own. Get rid of a significant percentage of the clothing, kitchen gadgets, toys, and backup items you own.

Minimalism has single-handedly given me more time, attention, and energy than any other time-management strategy I've tried to implement over the years. While I used to be constantly overwhelmed trying to manage the stuff in my home, minimalism offered us an entirely new approach. Remember: if it all feels like too much to manage, it probably is.

Minimalism led me to look at our cluttered home as a mathematical equation rather than an existential crisis of character. Instead of feeling overwhelmed by our stuff and then even more overwhelmed by our inability to manage it all, we can address it by asking this question: If something is taking up too much time, energy, or attention, can it be eliminated? Instead of feeling like we need to hustle harder, manufacture more hours, purchase a custom closet system, or order a new daily planner, we can first consider what to eliminate—or at the very least, drastically simplify. We don't have to spend our lives trying to become elite consumers of stuff.

The best part about minimalism is that "stuff" is only the beginning. Minimalism's time-producing capabilities reach far beyond your garage, drawers, and closets. It will also drastically reduce your time spent shopping, researching, and subsequently returning new purchases. You'll start spending less and less of your capacity cleaning, maintaining, and updating *things* and more time experiencing, enjoying, and savoring *life*. Put plainly, owning fewer material possessions means less time spent on your material possessions. And that's a beautiful thing.

Now, I'm aware that minimalism isn't everybody's cup of tea. I mean, personally, I think it could be; however, some of my closest friends and family assure me that it's not. Yet while minimalism per se isn't for everybody, the benefits of a clutter-free home are. The trouble is, getting there can be an uphill battle that often leaves people camping at the base instead of embarking on the climb.

Not only does decluttering take a good chunk of time and energy, *maintaining* your clutter-free home requires a shift in thinking. Just as social media companies are actively working to declare eminent domain over your attention, so are the makers of material possessions doing the same with your space and your bank account. In fact, these two entities are working in cahoots to lure you away from your present moment to sell you anything from an ideology to a new couch. We see an average of five thousand advertisements a day. Back in 1970, folks only had to endure five hundred.

Because of that, numbing out on social media isn't just a time waster or negative coping strategy. It can escalate into a money-waster as well. All we wanted were a few moments of silence—and the next thing you know we're adding some stranger's favorite sherpa overalls to our shopping cart. You didn't even know that item existed five minutes ago, but now you must have it.

Even now, after all these years of living as a more conscious consumer, when I'm stressed, I feel compelled to go buy something. But we don't have to succumb to the temptation of retail therapy. Instead, we can get in the habit of pausing to ask ourselves what's going on. Do I genuinely need these things, or am I avoiding conflict, hard work, or stress? Sometimes it's the former. Minimalist or not, we all need some things from time to time. All too often, however, I find it's the latter. It's our brain's way of avoiding a life stressor. *Ahhh! Packing and moving is hard. Home Goods, anyone?*

But resisting the urge to buy our way out of high-pressure situations will pay dividends in the future. Not only do we move through the stress faster by facing it head on, we also don't create more work for ourselves down the road by filling our homes with needless items we then have to manage.

Since I've already written an entire book specifically about going minimalist, I won't dive into all its principles here. Instead, we are going to talk about creating a clutter-free home as a method for better managing our busier seasons. Just as owning fewer things made our move across town easier, so can it lighten your load during commonly chaotic seasons.

You don't need more laundry to fold, appliances to put away, or décor to rearrange after bringing your first baby home from the hospital. When you've got multiple high schoolers in varsity sports, the last thing you need is a home that takes an entire Saturday to tidy up. Your limited capacity and margin should go toward activities that fill you up, not take more out of you. And I'm willing to bet that rearranging bathroom drawers and kitchen countertops wouldn't make the list of your favorite ways to spend that one wild and precious life of yours. You've got enough to do and plenty of places to go right now. The last thing you need is to be bossed around by inanimate objects that won't matter in the end.

GIVE YOUR FUTURE STRESSED-OUT SELF
THE GIFT OF A CLUTTER-FREE HOME

Reducing the number of material possessions in your home is like giving your future stressed-out self a glorious gift. I wish I had a foolproof, three-step approach to hand you that would guarantee you would never find yourself in over your head again. But we've both seen some things. We know that's not how being a person works.

What I'm proposing instead is that by reducing the clutter within your home, you can reduce your mental load and free up some time. We make time management so much harder on ourselves when we fill our physical space with stuff we don't need. The extra sweaters and redundant serving ware may have scratched your dopamine itch when you impulse-bought them. They may even provide you with a little "but what if I need it someday?" security blanket. But they're doing very little at this point to satisfy your craving for a meaningful life. Impulse shopping and trend hopping offer temporary relief for a much bigger issue buzzing beneath the figurative floorboards of your home.

Don't worry, within twenty-four hours of Raegan's middle-of-the-night encounter with the business end of a yellowjacket, we found a stellar father–son extermination team willing to tackle them head on. They went right to the source of that hive and rid our home of those yellowjackets once and for all. We haven't had to fight them off again since.

Now, the stuff littering your floors may just be the result of living with messy middle schoolers who think the living room floor is an extension of their bedroom closet. Been there. But keep a look out because it very well may be a warning sign that a too much stuff problem is brewing beneath the surface.

FIVE AREAS TO DECLUTTER ASAP

It's important to note that when you're in the middle of a busy season, the very last thing you have time for is a head-to-toe home purge. The extensive decluttering that minimalism typically initiates takes time—sometimes lots of it, depending on just how much stuff you've been holding on to. In fact, it took our family of five a full year to weed out the clutter from every nook and cranny and closet in our home. We simply had more excess stuff than excess minutes to address it all. If you're ready to make some major changes in your home as it pertains to material possessions, know that it won't happen overnight. You'll have to tackle it cabinet by cabinet, corner by corner, room by room, and then in larger strides as your busy seasons let up. It pays off in the end, but be sure to give yourself plenty of grace to tackle the clutter at a pace that works for the season you're in.

That said, for immediate reprieve, we're going to address five day-to-day areas of the home prone to clutter. Now you may be thinking: "*Every* area of my home is prone to clutter, Rachelle." Without an intentional approach to purchasing and accumulating material possessions, it doesn't take long for those somewhat cluttered corners to morph into a full-on clutter infestation.

Whether you dive all the way in to minimalism or simply implement a few of its principles here and there, minimalism will drastically reduce your mental load. Despite the way minimalism has been marketed to us on social media, it's *not* a picture-perfect, one-size-fits-all method for creating beautiful, trending homes. Minimalism doesn't have a reputation to uphold. Instead, it's a mindset and approach to life that supports the stage of life you're in by helping you to curate a living space that serves you in this season. By eradicating the inessential from your home, you can create a reprieve from the chaos rather than inflicting further damage. Let's take a look at five high-clutter areas to tackle sooner than later in order to reduce your mental load and create more capacity.

1. Wardrobe

If you can only get to one area of your home right now, I'd recommend tackling your clothing. Not only does a simplified wardrobe leave you with fewer articles of clothing to launder, fold, and gather from around the home, it lightens your decision-making load as well. Getting ready in the morning is so much easier when you have fewer articles of clothing to choose from.

On top of all that, you just might find a simpler wardrobe transforming how you use your free time as well. Our culture has turned shopping for new clothes into a form of entertainment rather than a utilitarian task. Because of that, we spend our precious free time adding more clutter to our homes. While it works out well for retail companies, it's doing little good for your time, energy, and bank account. When I stopped shopping for new clothes "just for the fun of it," it freed up a surprising amount of time and money to invest in more quality activities and experiences. Instead of packing my closet full of fun finds, I have more time to be outdoors, read, write, and spend time with my family.

It doesn't end with clothing, either. Becoming a more conscious consumer of clothes led me to become a more conscious consumer of other things as well. Things like home décor, kitchen gadgets, kids' toys, and hobby gear are all things I now second-guess before purchasing. Things don't need to be updated and replaced nearly as often as the Westernized world has gotten in the habit of doing. In fact, getting us to feel compelled to update possessions is a marketing strategy known as *perceived obsolescence*. It's meant to keep us on our toes, ready to shop for new things as trends change. The older I get, though, the more I've come to realize what goes around comes around. Shoes and pants I rocked as a teenager are currently back on the shelves of the very stores I once shopped in. It's not just a blast from the past; it's proof that many trends are cyclical. If you wait long enough, the style you love is bound to make an appearance again at some point.

While frustrating, this is good news. You can opt out of the trend game. You can wear what you love and ditch the rest so your mental load can find the reprieve it needs. When talking to others about what holds them back from decluttering their wardrobes, I find that the biggest hurdle tends to be the sunk cost bias, which we addressed back in chapter 6. Not only does sunk cost bias keep us from quitting activities that aren't working, it causes us to hold on to our excess material possessions simply because of how much they cost us upfront.

When you find yourself paralyzed by the sunk cost bias, take a minute to mentally time travel one hundred years into the future. Where is that itchy overpriced sweater now? Do you see it? If it's lucky, it's on the vintage rack of your local thrift store. But more likely, it's in a landfill somewhere. Decluttering the stuff we don't need isn't financially wasteful or even environmentally unfriendly. *Purchasing* it may have been, but the discarding of it is simply inevitable. All you're doing when decluttering your home is getting to the future faster. Wastefulness comes into play when we don't change our overconsumption habits going forward. When we declutter our closets only to fill them again with clothing we don't need, *that* is wasteful. Learning to live with fewer articles of clothing than you've been used to is both environmentally friendly and financially sound. One way to do that is to create a capsule wardrobe.

A capsule wardrobe is a small number of clothes that can, to some degree, all be mixed and matched and worn together. This means instead of owning a variety of colors and patterns, you stick with a smaller palette of colors, so everything matches. This way you'll be able to create a variety of different outfits with ease each day.

Sick of digging through a pile of your child's mismatched clothing every morning before school? If you're a parent, consider creating a capsule wardrobe for your kids as well. In my experience, with a capsule wardrobe, you can even send your four-year-old to their closet to pick out an outfit on their own and they won't come out dressed like a Jackson Pollock painting.

2. Kitchen

The kitchen is an easily cluttered space, loaded with preconceived ideas, habits, and misconceptions about the quantity and variety of items we should keep in our homes. Because of that, decluttering it can be more difficult than the other areas of your home. Tackling the kitchen is usually easier once you have experience decluttering a few less complicated areas of the home first.

That said, the kitchen is the most frequently used space in the home. Creating a clutter-free kitchen will have a wide-reaching impact that ripples through your home and daily routines.

I'm often asked about kitchen counters. "How do you clear kitchen counters? Mine are loaded with appliances and papers!" The secret—clutter-free cabinets! You can clear your counters with ease once you're able to store the items you use *inside* your cabinets instead of on your counters. Of course, this starts with ruthlessly decluttering those cabinets. If your cabinets are anything like mine were, they house some seriously inessential items. I was holding onto appliances, serving ware, and pans we used rarely to never. Once you start clearing your cabinets of the things you don't need, everything you do need will find a home.

Here are a few areas to consider decluttering:

- **Spices:** Spices creep up on you. One day you have a normal-person number of spices for the recipes you actually make, and the next your spice cabinet has overflowed into three others. Suddenly you're storing more spices than a World Buffet kitchen. Eliminating the spices you don't use will free up a lot of wasted space in your kitchen. I like to look at my spices the same way I do my clothing—like a capsule. Which spices can I keep to make the widest variety of dishes with the least amount of clutter? Just because you used a random spice for that one dish that one time doesn't mean you need to keep it until well after it expires.
- **Storage containers:** Storage container lids are like the missing socks of the kitchen: somehow they go missing when there's literally no place to go. Why are they never with the containers themselves? I'm convinced there's a

trapdoor in the back of our lazy Susan. So first things first: ditch the storage containers that can't be assembled together. They are relatively useless without a lid anyway. Once the mismatched ones are gone, consider how many you need to own at all. If you've got stacks upon stacks of storage containers that haven't held actual food in months, donate the excess. Those things take up a lot of precious cabinet real estate.

- **Kitchen appliances and serving ware:** I've lumped these together because the decluttering process for both is quite similar. Do you have appliances or serving ware you don't use? Get rid of them. Do you have appliances or serving ware that can perform similar tasks? Let go of the duplicates. Perhaps you don't need three dishes large enough to serve a turkey. I mean, assuming you don't cook three turkeys every Thanksgiving. Do you have a variety of blenders? How many smoothies do you need to make at one time? Consider letting go of the duplicate items to free up some much-needed space. Now if you're holding onto some serving pieces because they are heirlooms, by all means, keep them. I'm not here for your sentimental items. At least not in this book. I'm willing to bet, though, that your kitchen isn't cluttered solely with sentimental serving ware. It's cluttered because of all the other other stuff you're holding on to. Look around for the items that are not using your precious cabinet space well, and let go of those things first.
- **Coffee mugs:** These get a bad rap. It seems every minimalist out there wants you to declutter your mismatched coffee mugs or pare down to just a couple. After all, how many mugs do you really need, right? But I am not one of those minimalists. I love coffee mugs. Preferably of the thrifted, vintage kind. I'm a sucker for finding a 1970s coffee mug at a garage sale that costs a quarter. The point of

minimalism isn't to make your home *look* minimalist with simple, white, matching coffee mugs. There is no predetermined list of inessential items all minimalists agree you should ditch. This is *your* living space. How can it best serve you and your family? That said, if you're not weirdly into eclectic coffee mugs like I am, they should absolutely be the first to go. If you are, don't let some arbitrary minimalist rule hold you back from decluttering the other areas of your home. You can have your cake and eat it too. You can keep your fun coffee mugs and live in a clutter-free home.

3. Toiletries

Toiletries seem to reproduce in our bathroom drawers. Maybe all the missing storage container lids have been shape-shifting into makeup samples, five-year-old lotions, and hotel room toiletries. Bathroom drawers are highly prone to clutter. My favorite method for pruning toiletries and beauty products is to analyze them after returning home from a trip.

Have you taken any trips recently? What did you pack? The essentials, right? Only the products you need every day. Let travel filter what you keep and what you eliminate. Ask yourself this: If I was going on vacation, would I pack this? Do I really need to keep four different curl creams and two separate blow dryers? Now, I don't know what you do and don't need, so I won't try to speculate. In my experience, though, you're never going to get around to using *all* the bath products you've accumulated. If they wouldn't travel with you, perhaps they can be eliminated entirely.

4. Coat Closet

Whether you have an entire room, a small closet, or merely a coat rack housing your outdoor gear and school backpacks, simplifying this area can make getting out the door in the morning far easier. Depending on the climate you live in and the outdoor hobbies you participate in, the amount of outdoor gear you own will vary.

One of the fastest ways to clutter up a space like this is by holding onto gear you don't need. Extra shoes, redundant coats, and a basket of only left-hand children's mittens will quickly clutter up your coat closet. By reducing the amount of outdoor gear, you can streamline this space and make it work more efficiently for you and your family. If you've ever spent a Saturday morning digging through tennis shoes nobody wears in search of a missing shin guard before a soccer game, then you've experienced overconsumption-induced anxiety. Those "but what if we need them someday?" shoes you're saving? They aren't making your life easier today. They are simply making it more difficult to find the items you need right now.

5. Nightstand

If all you have the capacity to declutter right now is the contents on your nightstand, do it. You'd be surprised by how calming a clutter-free bedside table can be when you are rising in the morning and going to bed at night. If you're too deep in a busy season right now to tackle the larger areas of your home, start here. It's a relatively small task that reaps big rewards.

In time, creating even just a small clutter-free corner in your home can ripple throughout the rest of it. The thought of decluttering our *entire* space can feel so overwhelming that it keeps us from getting started at all. Sometimes you must give yourself the opportunity to experience the benefits of less in small doses before you find the strength to work for it everywhere else.

A clutter-free home isn't just aesthetically pleasing. It can mean the difference between thriving during a busier season of life or just surviving it. Decluttering as a time-management strategy is ultimately about giving a home to the items you use daily. When you can easily locate the things you need, your day will run smoother. The more stuff we own, the more time, energy, and attention we need to dedicate to that stuff. I'm willing to bet that's the last thing you care to devote your limited capacity to.

TIP FOR BEING BUSY WELL:
USE GROWTH SPURTS

Decluttering your home is complicated enough. Add in the wants, needs, and opinions of your children, and it can quickly start to feel like more work than it's worth. But I assure you: it's worth every drop of effort. One secret is to harness the power of the growth spurt.

Say your six-year-old has more dresses than she'd ever need yet panics at the thought of letting any of them go. Maybe your son is currently obsessed with [insert coolest new trending toy]. You're realizing it's all too much to manage, but you can't seem to talk them into donating a single thing. Instead of stressing about it, fighting over which toys to donate, talking yourself in circles, or sneaking things out in the middle of the night, wait. Give it a minute, or more like six months. One day they are going to wake up and those dresses won't fit, the shoe collection will be too tight, and the favorite toys will be disregarded for the next new thing. Use those changes in interest and leaps in leg length to your advantage.

When they need new clothes that fit, buy fewer. When birthdays or the holidays roll around, pare back the number of gifts you normally give. It doesn't have to be a drastic change all at once, but over time, you'll decrease how much stuff they own—without the battle.

CHAPTER TWELVE

Be on Your Mat

The Art of Undistracted Living

At the ripe old age of forty-one, I learned to downhill ski. In the spirit of #experiencesoverthings, we had given our kids ski lessons for Christmas. Since we couldn't very well send a seven-year-old up a ski lift by herself, Paul and I would need to learn as well. After a two-hour lesson and a few pride-swallowing spills, I got the hang of it—ish.

One crowded Sunday afternoon, just a few weeks after first learning to ski, Paul, Raegan, and I patiently waited for our turn to go up the lift together. If you've ever been on a ski lift, you know there is a bit of a procedure to getting on and off. When getting on the lift, you've got to time it just right so that you're shuffling forward before your chair cuts you off. Then, when exiting the lift, you've got to get off and out of the way before it knocks you over. It's organized chaos, but once you get the hang of it, it's not as terrifying as I just made it sound.

As the chair approached us from behind, I sat down on it, like I always do. However, this time, something was noticeably off from the start. I quickly realized there was, in fact, no chair beneath my buns. Only my elbows and upper back had found the seat before the lift began to push me forward and upward. I had sat too soon.

Paul tried to pull me onto the chair, but his skis were caught on mine and were therefore simultaneously holding me down. It was a lost cause. I was being dragged up the ski lift during the busiest day of the season, while dozens of other skiers watched from the lift line.

In that moment, I had two choices: keep trying to shimmy my body onto this seat, or let go before I got carried too high in the air. I chose to cut my losses and let go. The inattentive lift operator eventually noticed the body on the ground and hit the stop button on the lift. I slowly looked up to see Paul and Raegan another fifteen or so feet ahead of me, looking back with their jaws on the ground, holding in laughter. Thank goodness I had let go or I would have been dangling in the air beneath them.

I just sat there for a few seconds, absolutely mortified, wishing the good Lord would return at that moment in a flame of glory to offer a distraction. The last thing I wanted to do was turn and face the crowd of strangers behind me. No such luck, though. The only way out of this mess I'd gotten myself into was going to be through it.

I popped off my skis, gathered my poles, and made the long, mortifying walk of shame back to the chairlift to start over. The whole line remained paused, everybody silently staring as I pulled myself together and got on the chair alone.

For better or worse, this is how I learn. Common sense would tell you how important it is to pay close attention to the chair as it approaches, to lock eyes with it before attempting to sit down. But common sense isn't always the best teacher. You know what is? Utter humiliation. What can I say? I'm a learn-the-hard-way kind of gal. Since that fateful winter day, I haven't sat on a chairlift without that event coming to mind. I henceforth will forever turn, look at the chairlift, and grab the back of the seat prior to sitting on it. Being dragged up a chairlift has that effect on you.

During chaotic seasons, it's easy to lose sight of the things that need our undivided attention. One minute we're "soaking up the moment," and the next we're being knocked down and dragged along, hoping someone will hit the brakes on our behalf. While excessive screen time may be the largest and most current enemy of the attentive life, it's not the only offender. While the smartphone has made it significantly more difficult to stay focused and in the present moment, we've always been looking for a way out. Social media is just the latest distraction. Sure, ditching our phones for the day will give us a bit of a head start. But if we aren't careful, we can take that blank space and fill it with a myriad of other distractions. Let's dive into a few.

WORRY

If you're anything like me, you're prone to worrying your way through an event without being truly present for much of it. Instead of soaking up what's happening around us, we become anxious. We might start to worry we don't belong here, stress that we overshared, or grow concerned that something is going to give at any moment. When our brains function like this long enough, we don't even realize we're doing it. It's just the backdrop for every scene we live through.

Next to my phone, worry just may be the largest distraction in my life. I'm not talking about clinical anxiety, which is another beast entirely. I'm referring to those of us with a tendency to overthink and make decisions based off worst-case scenarios rather than facts. We've got rich imaginations when it comes to the many things that could go wrong. While we still desire a full life, caked with adventure and new experiences, our overthinking threatens to claim much of our mental energy before we ever have the chance to partake. Instead of savoring the moment, we're off on a mental mission to prevent potential catastrophe. We'll formulate a rebuttal for a conflict that hasn't yet occurred, create multiple itineraries to help us avoid a negative outcome, and implement a plan of action to guarantee safe passage through life. As if that's at all possible. It's exhausting.

I know I'm not alone in this. Here's the good news, though: worry can become your superpower. Just as our pain receptors keep us safe, so can worry be a vital tool. Yet the narrative around worry tends to be a negative one. In the movies, being a worrier makes you the wimp, never the hero. Always the one slowing everyone down.

While studies have shown we can worry our way into an early grave, that same bent toward worry can be the very thing that saves the day. It's easy to compare our own tentative and hesitant decision-making process to someone else's more haphazard or risk-defying approach and assume that we're the ones who need to pull it together. Sure, the safer, more reluctant path may not sell well in Hollywood. That's true. But when we look beyond the cinematography to better understand how real world-changing innovators function, we find they tend to hedge their bets by taking the safer route more than you'd think.

In his book *Originals*, Adam Grant points out that the entrepreneurs who move the world forward with original ideas may be more risk averse than they appear on the outside. "We find that entrepreneurs are significantly more risk averse than the general population," he writes. "Originals do vary in their attitudes toward risk. Some are skydiving gamblers; others are penny-pinching germaphobes. To become original, you've got to try something new, which means accepting some measure of risk. But the most successful originals are not the daredevils who leap before they look. They are the ones who reluctantly tiptoe to the edge of cliff, calculate the rate of descent, triple-check their parachutes, and set up a safety net at the bottom just in case."

Don't get me wrong: worry can cause us to miss out on enjoyment, adventure, and purpose. There's a difference between raising a red flag from time to time and setting up permanent camp underneath a banner of them. We could calculate that "rate of descent" over and over until we've entirely missed the opportunity to jump.

Instead, we can capitalize on the bright side of worry. We can use it to be calculated, strategic, insightful, and thoughtful. Then, instead of getting stuck resolving every potential issue, asking, "But what if this or that goes wrong?" we can follow up with a better what-if question: "But what if it *doesn't*?"

If you find yourself headed down the rabbit hole of worry, pause and consider the possibility that those worst-case scenarios will, more than likely, never come to fruition. I'm a big fan of a good backup plan, but be careful how much time you devote to developing and perfecting them. Odds are pretty good you won't need them anyway. If you find yourself stuck creating backup plans for your backup plans, jar yourself awake by asking that one follow-up question: What if nothing goes wrong? I've found it helps me stop borrowing trouble from tomorrow so I can set my mind where it is right now.

PERFECTIONISM

Perfectionism is another common distraction that causes us to miss out on being present. Instead of rolling with the messy moments and inevitable changes that accompany real life, we exert an excessive amount of effort to execute every moment with precision. We get wrapped up in micromanaging our current circumstances and put undue pressure on ourselves to plan flawless events or be the mom who volunteers for literally *everything*. We prioritize putting our best face forward at the expense of every other part of us. We'll declutter our home as a means to simplify it, but rather than enjoying the space and time we've created, we find ourselves even more distracted. *Did we declutter enough? Should I renovate now to make it trendier?*

Perfectionism forces us to ignore the season we're in in order to meet unrealistic, arbitrary expectations. One area highly prone to perfectionism is the way in which we try to replicate family traditions. We take a holiday, make it magical, and then assume that for it to remain magical, we must remake that same moment in the exact same way, over and over every year, for all of eternity, amen. Instead of simply enjoying events or holidays as they unfold, we make it our job to copy and paste.

Early on in my motherhood, I made our family a DIY Advent calendar. I strung rows of twine on the wall and hung twenty-five little brown envelopes on it from red, green, and white clothespins. The contents of each envelope varied. Some held a Bible verse to memorize, others an act of kindness to perform, and a few contained a tiny tchotchke or a small treat to devour.

During the first year, this Advent calendar was exciting and adorable. The next year, it was cute, but it quickly tired me out. I found myself eager for Christmas to arrive, but mostly because I was done trying to fill each of those little envelopes with creative ideas. By year number three, I started to loathe it. *What have I gotten myself into?* There I stood, before a holiday tradition meant to point us toward the birth of Christ, feeling compelled to toss the whole thing in the trash.

Instead of acknowledging that this activity had run its course, I looked at it as a permanent member of the family. A holiday tradition I must replicate until death do us part. Since it was now a "tradition," I was responsible for carrying it out every December.

The same way sentiment isn't locked inside a family heirloom or travel souvenir, neither is tradition beholden to the activity itself. Tradition and sentiment are found in experiencing connection. The activity is simply the vehicle. Holiday traditions don't need to occur the exact same way, every single year, for them to feel like successes. The joy isn't contingent upon what you're able to squeeze in, check off, or pull together.

That's a lot of unnecessary pressure we've been putting on ourselves. And we're the ones who pay the highest price. We miss out on experiencing the joy in the everyday moments when we're too distracted by all the should-dos and have-to-dos.

MENTALLY RUNNING THROUGH TO-DO LISTS

There's a time to get stuff done, and a time to accomplish absolutely nothing. Yes, doing nothing is actually something in and of itself—an important something at that. When we waste our downtime by mentally running through our to-do lists, thinking ahead about how we'll execute the rest of the week, or by manufacturing new projects to tackle, we end up getting nothing accomplished. And meanwhile, we also fail to *do nothing*.

My husband has a hard time doing nothing. On his days home, he always feels compelled to work on some sort of project. I, on the other hand, am quite good at doing nothing. It's my mind that wanders. It actively moves through to-do lists, recalls appointments I forgot were nearing, and initiates a bunch of projects in my head that I'll likely never get to. While it's easy to throw judgment at my busy-body husband who's out spontaneously sweeping the garage, a busy *brain* can drain your capacity just as fast. I mean, at least he has something to show for it at the end of the day.

Take a good look at the way you're using your limited free time. Do you find yourself just as mentally drained after a day of rest or leisure as you do on your average workday? It may be because your mind is still hard at work, micromanaging family conflicts, creating new task lists, or pondering the areas of your home you'd like to update. The next thing you know you're at the hardware store buying new light fixtures, and maybe a couple baby chicks while you're at it—even though you *meant* to spend your day off baking cookies and beating your teenagers in ping-pong. "Divide and conquer" may work when relying on your spouse to help coordinate sporting event logistics, but it's an ineffective method for just one person. You can't refill and pour out at the same time. Remember: you're not an octopus.

Years ago, I was in a yoga class when the instructor spouted off this short, sweet sentence as she moved through the room: "If you're going to be on your mat, be on your mat."

This one line has never left me. On that cold winter day, she was telling the class that if you're going to drive all the way here to be present in body, you might as well be present in mind as well. If you're here, do the work that being here requires of you. It was a broad statement made to the entire class, but I'm certain she was looking my way when she said it.

I don't think a week passes now that this line doesn't reverberate in my mind. I'll think to myself: if you're going to take the day to rest, Rachelle, take the day to rest. If you're going to make a fire and read a book, don't pick up your phone as well. If you're going to drive to the gym, go all in. If you're going to take your kids to the beach, *be* at the beach. If you're going to play checkers, ping-pong, or Uno with your kids, be there in both body and mind. Stop thinking about dinner, laundry, work, or the book you must write, when you've set aside predetermined quality time for the activities that fill you up.

CONFLICT

I'm an oldest sister. Oldest sisters don't sit on the sidelines watching conflict unfold. No, we get all up in your business to try and solve it for you. It's not in our nature to mind our own business. We're much more comfortable taking on the posture of problem solver. The trouble isn't with our desire to step in and go to bat for those we love. The trouble is when we confuse *caring* with *carrying*. When we bear others' burdens in a way that leaves us unable to reengage in our own daily lives when we get back home.

Just because you care (and you do deeply care) doesn't mean something is yours to carry. Just because a crisis is underway doesn't mean you have to make it your whole personality. To all the older sisters out there, both the literal and metaphorical ones, it's time to set some healthier boundaries.

Big sisters tend to make everyone's problems our own. All too often we set up permanent residence in someone else's chaotic season at the expense of our own physical, mental, and emotional energy. By all means, be the big sister you were created to be. Step in, help out, and shoulder the weight for a bit. But don't forget to set it down again. Say it with me: "Not my circus, not my monkeys. Not my circus, not my monkeys."

The older I get, the more I've come to learn that we can spare ourselves a whole lot of mental fatigue and keep our own reservoirs full longer when we keep healthy boundaries between caring about what someone is going through and carrying what isn't ours to carry.

CHRONIC OVERCOMMITMENT

We've established that we're going to have full calendars from time to time. And we know that those chaotic calendars can even be a beautiful gift when we've simplified everything within them and around them—a sign of meaningful connections and purposeful work. A calendar that remains too full for too long, however, can be our undoing.

I'll keep this brief, because we've already addressed this in previous sections, but being busy well depends on the margin we make and maintain within and after those busy seasons.

When we're chronically overcommitted, we're more likely to find ourselves drowning in the hurried life. And within the hurried life, we're more prone to distraction.

Since the nurse in me just can't help it, let's compare it to post-surgical pain management, shall we? It's far easier to keep your pain levels at bay on the front end, by staying on top of pain medications, than it is to try and bring excruciating pain levels down by playing catch-up later. It takes more time and medication to lower pain levels if you've let your pain grow out of control. In the same way, preventing overcommitment on the front end is a far easier endeavor than trying to walk it back. It's much more difficult to wiggle your way out of too many activities and responsibilities *after* you've committed to them. Or, just as it's far easier to cut your losses and let go early on when dangling from a ski lift, so is it easier to say no to things before you've committed to them.

Every ounce of space you create and maintain in your calendar offers an opportunity to be fully present and fill back up. It's when we leave our phones behind, push the lingering to-do lists from our minds, ignore the pull toward making it all perfect, and leave worry by the wayside that we can *be* exactly where we are.

WHY BEING PRESENT IS SO IMPORTANT

My littlest has FOMO like no other. Actually, it's not so much a fear of missing out as it is resentment over *having* missed out. It's ROHMO, really.

When you're the youngest in the family, you aren't in all the family photos. And even if you are in them, you don't necessarily have the same memories as your older siblings do. There are inside jokes you don't get and events you napped through. After all, you were just a baby. When we're reminiscing about something that happened BA (before Amelia), you'll notice her glaring at you from across the room, arms folded across her chest. It's a comically depressing sight. She *hates* hearing about the things she missed when she wasn't even born yet.

A few summers back we took our annual trip to Van Buren State Park on the shore of Lake Michigan. Thankfully there hadn't been a recent Ekman spiral to sabotage our plans, so the lake water was the perfect temperature. We spent the day climbing sand dunes, eating our weight in Cheetos, taking turns judging underwater handstand contests, and combing the shore for beach glass. It was just like one of those #PureMichigan advertisement kind of days.

At one point, five-year-old Amelia was trying to float on her back, so I stood above her, supporting her head so it wouldn't dip under with the waves. She looked up at me with a face of pure contentment and said, "I love these good ole days."

Talk about a core memory. I'll never forget it, and I hope you don't either. Particularly the word *these*. *These* good ole days. She wasn't recalling memories from years past or anticipating what tomorrow would hold. She was fully present, aware that the moment she was in right now was a good ole day. One she didn't intend to miss.

Identifying the good ole days, though, can feel more like trying to see fog close up. You might be standing directly in the middle of a foggy yard, but you can only see the fog that's off in the distance. Never directly at your feet. At your feet, it looks just like every other day.

This is why it's so important to live each day like it's a good ole day: because it likely is. You just won't know it until there's a bit more distance between you and the present moment. Instead of savoring these good ole days, we often let hurry become a way of life. We tell ourselves we'll be in a better position to savor the moment when our schedule lets up in a few weeks, or once the school year comes to an end. Yet during certain seasons of life, that isn't how it unfolds. Instead, we enter the next phase only to find ourselves somehow busier than the last, looking off in the distance for the next moment of reprieve. What if we stopped looking ahead with anticipation, or regretfully in the rear-view mirror, and instead simply started assuming that the moments at our feet are the ones we've been holding out for? It's easy to look back on a series of memories and wish you'd made more space for them when you had the chance. But here's the good news: those may have been the good ole days, but so are these, the days you're living right now. Maybe they aren't quite what you expected, or they've come with more chaos than you thought they would, but that doesn't make being present for them any less important.

The good ole days are happening all around us, even within our average weekdays. When we grab hold of this truth like a five-year-old bobbing up and down with the waves, we'll start missing out on fewer and fewer of them. Let's not wait until seasons pass to sift through our moments and then slap a Top-40 label on the ones we think mattered most. Instead, let them all matter. Let them all grow you, push you, fill your bucket, leave you empty and occasionally humiliated. After all, moments of the "chairlift spill" variety make for great stories later. As the lyrics of AJR go, "100 bad days make 100 good stories."

In the moment, falling off the ski lift wasn't what I'd consider a "good ole day." At the time, it was just flat-out mortifying. Today, however, it's in the archives of our family experiences right alongside the picture-perfect ones. I've recounted that story any number of times to my kids as well as to students I work with at school: "So if I can survive the embarrassment of falling off a chairlift in front of a large crowd of experienced skiers, then you can certainly [insert relevant situation]."

Don't let overcommitment, worry, perfectionism, excessive screen time, overconsumption of stuff, or the promise of future reprieve leave you looking back wishing you'd been more present for the good ole days you're in right this very minute.

LOCKED ON

As a new skier, I *know* I need to be locked on when I head down a hill. I'm very aware that skiing requires my full attention. Falling off a chairlift when you're hanging just a few feet off the ground only hurts your pride. Losing control and slamming into a tree? *That* will have real consequences.

In much the same way, being present during the *significant* moments is relatively easy. It's easier to be present when you're at the beach without cell service. Or when you're holding your first grand-child, watching your daughter graduate, or sitting in a blind on opening day of deer season with your son (light-up boots and all). You *know* those moments are significant enough to warrant your undivided attention.

But doing so during the ordinary moments, when life feels cha-otic, is much harder. When you're in the thick of it, running kids to various practices, cooking dinner for toddler-sized food critics, or working extra hours to make ends meet as the rising cost of living pulls those ends further and further apart? That's next level. The more mundane moments that matter can get overshadowed by the responsibility and fatigue of being a person.

Yet, living a present and intentional life doesn't require an escape route. By leaning into those chaotic seasons of life, we can start panning for the small but valuable golden moments that matter and replenish our capacity right where we are. It's just a matter of finding the meaningful moments available to us in the midst of our day-to-day lives. They're there. In my experience, you simply need to know what to look for.

TIP FOR BEING BUSY WELL: DESIGNATE A DECIDER

Sometimes the margin on our calendars is abundant, but it's our mental margin that is lacking. We've got so many decisions and tasks weighing on us that being present feels like a lost cause. If it feels like you're just one more question away from ruin, you may be suffering from decision fatigue. This is when we're overwhelmed by the many decisions we have to make or paralyzed by the number of options we have to sift through in order to decide. Being a person comes with lots of decisions. With each person you're caring for comes the added weight of making decisions on their behalf as well.

An effective strategy for avoiding or reducing decision fatigue is to designate a decider for the more inconsequential decisions in life. I have several experts lined up to make the decisions I'm bad at making. I've got a paint-color friend who makes the majority of my home decor decisions and a fashionable friend because sometimes I'm too frumpy for my own good. I've got myself a vegetable-garden friend, a maple-syrup-making friend, a recipe guru on Instagram, and even a bird friend. (I mean, you never know when you'll have a bird-related question. I'm in my forties now, you know. I hear birding is basically the next stage of development.)

Consider the areas of your life where you can delegate your decision-making. I could stress for weeks and never manage to select the perfect shade of warm white for my walls. But one visit from my friend Elise and the decision is made. Bam.

CHAPTER THIRTEEN

Be Present

The Art of Creating Meaningful Moments
Out of Everyday Life

One of my favorite times of the year is morel season. Morels are a local wild mushroom that can be incredibly hard to find. While you may stumble upon one in your backyard one year, there's no guarantee you'll find more there in the future. They can be very temperamental. On top of being elusive, their growing window is extremely short lived. In fact, the opportunity to find morel mushrooms lasts roughly three weeks, give or take. That's it. Once they're gone, you've got to wait until next year.

You might think, given my morel enthusiasm, that I bring home an abundance of them every season. Quite the opposite. Historically, I'm terrible at finding morels. In fact, during my first eight years as a morel mushroom hunter, I found approximately four. Not four a year, mind you: four mushrooms *in total*. Most seasons were a total bust. That doesn't stop me from looking, though. If I've got even just one free hour of daylight while the morels are popping, into the woods I'll go.

Paul once offered to stop at the market and just buy me a pound. These bougie little mushrooms can run upward of $80 a pound.

Still, he saw purchasing morels as a better use of our resources than my foraging, which often yielded, well, none. Why spend hours and hours scouring the ground when you could just buy a few and be done already? The math wasn't mathing for him.

To me, however, this wasn't about the math. I refused his offer, because where's the fun in that? Besides, I wasn't ready to admit defeat. I love *looking* for morels as much as actually finding them. If I didn't thoroughly enjoy the search, I would have given up long ago.

Despite the slim odds of finding morel mushrooms, I look forward to the search like a child does Christmas morning. If conditions are perfect and the timing is right, I've even pulled Raegan out of school to help me look. Her eyesight rivals the nose of a blood hound. Taking Raegan to look for morels is the equivalent of hiring a tracking dog to trail your deer. Lucky for me, I only have to pay her in root beer, quality time, and a missed class or two.

A couple of years ago, while lamenting to my forager friend Kristy over the fact that I continually come out empty handed, she shared a photo with me of her haul for the week. The photo she sent me, though, didn't include one single morel mushroom. Instead, her countertop was covered with a variety of other delicious wild mushrooms. She had found chicken of the woods, pheasant back mushrooms, and a huge cluster of golden oysters. I had never even heard of some of these before. I had had no idea there were so many edible mushrooms ripe for the picking in the same woods where I was hyperfocused on just one.

In my quest to find what I perceived as the best, rarest, most elusive delicacy, I was stepping right over a bounty of others. Now that I know what to look for, I rarely come out of the woods empty-handed. When I keep both my eyes and my options open, there's always something delicious to be found. Morels or no morels, I'm cooking up local fungi every spring. In fact, my family would tell you the plentiful golden oyster mushroom just may be the *superior* wild mushroom. When pan fried in butter with salt and pepper they taste like little golden, crispy chips of goodness.

When it comes to making time for the things that fill us up—whether that be self-care, quality time with the people we love, or purposeful work we long to invest in—it's easy to assume those opportunities are few and far between. That it requires a sabbatical to start an organization, or that the stars need align so we can participate in an elaborate adventure. Rarely are we looking for the small, seemingly insignificant moments that ultimately matter even more. We step right over top of the things happening every day in hot pursuit of those once-in-a-lifetime moments. We miss out on the abundance of little ways to replenish our reserves, connect with our loved ones, and experience adventure while we're hoping to stumble across the grander ones.

But a full life isn't the one spent living vacation to vacation. It's not about accruing enough paid time off to fill up in one big gulp—and then waiting a full year to do it all over again. No, a full life takes what it can find in each season. Busy or slow. Chaotic or calm. Stressful or relaxed. Once you begin to resist the hurried life, by holding tight to whatever margin you've got and eliminating as many distractions as possible, you'll start to spot the plethora of simpler moments hiding in plain sight. Don't be surprised if you begin to realize the elusive ones are a bit overrated anyway. Those average, everyday moments just may end up being your favorite ones of all.

It's one thing to know we need to be present in order to savor the moment. Actually being present, however, takes a degree of intentionality and focus we often lack when in a chaotic season of life. Here are a few strategies to help you better position yourself to find and enjoy the moments that matter.

1. KNOW WHAT YOU'RE LOOKING FOR

Instead of solely looking for the more grandiose moments of rest, quality time, adventure, and self-care, keep your eyes peeled for the small ones. I know it sounds cheesy, but something as simple as the sun hitting my face as I drag our trash can from the street back up to our house can have a remarkably soul-filling effect—if I let it. Catching one of my kids' funny one-liners or laughing at an inside joke with my husband while the kids try to figure out what's so funny: such moments accrue like compound interest. And we didn't even have to leave our own property, let alone the country. You'll be surprised by how filling those understated moments are when you're attentive to them.

Raegan and I attended a morel mushroom hunting seminar at our local library (I told you we're diehards). One of the strategies presented as a way to spot more morels is to intermittently glance down at a photo of a morel mushroom while you're out looking for them. The idea is that it will prime your brain with what morels look like so your eyes will more easily spot them on the ground. One gentleman raised his hand to share that he keeps a small, wood-carved morel with him when he looks. He cups it with his hand in his pocket, occasionally glancing down at it to remind his brain of what it's looking for.

Think back to your most recent, average, good-ole-day kind of moment. Remember how it looked, what it felt like. Then let it inform what you're looking for as you scour your week for more of them. Keep your eyes peeled for small moments of connection with the people you love. Perhaps even put a photo or reminder of that moment as your phone's lock screen. Hey, if we're compulsively checking our phone, at least we can make it work for us instead of against us.

2. ELIMINATE THE DISTRACTIONS YOU CAN

If you've ever sold your home, you know how important first impressions are. Somehow, we managed to sell our house with a half-eaten pie tucked beneath our living room couch.

One day, while packing and prepping our home for an important showing, I was stress-eating half of a strawberry-rhubarb pie my mother-in-law had generously dropped off. I turned to Jameson with a mouthful of pie and said, "Jameson, here! Hide this pie from me."

As with gummy bears and my cellphone, I needed a little distance from that pie or I'd consume every last bite of it. I then spent the remainder of the day cleaning my little heart out, completely forgetting about that pie—*which, after all, was the goal.*

I left the home later that day, proud of our hard work, with that half-eaten pie hidden beneath the living room couch, fork still inside it. My husband and realtor sister didn't find it nearly as funny as I did when they learned of our real estate gaffe, *days later.*

But it worked, right? I was able to focus on cleaning and avoided stress eating an entire pie in one sitting, because out of sight, out of mind, out of reach. Ideally, we would have remembered to put the pie in the fridge before exiting the home. Still, it got the job done. And who knows? Maybe the subtle scent of strawberry-rhubarb pie sealed the deal for our buyers.

Just as pain and worry are your body's way of responding to dangerous stimuli, so are overstimulation and distraction warning signs that perhaps you need a little proximity from the stressor. It's your body's way of telling you something needs to give. When you have zero time to recharge or you're finding it difficult to be present, that's likely exactly what your body needs most.

Creating distance doesn't just apply to phones, gummy bears, and strawberry-rhubarb pie. Cancel any plans you can, walk away from the disastrous kitchen, leave the laundry for another day, and cancel the after-school playdate you never should have committed to in the first place. It's time to offload whatever you can.

When you're overwhelmed or simply in a busier season of life, imagine yourself on a sinking boat, just trying to make it back to shore. The best way to ensure you don't sink before hitting land is to start tossing the heavier things overboard to lighten your load.

What are the things that weigh on you? What do you need to remove from arm's reach? When you're busy, you may find you have a lower threshold for the amount you can carry. That's okay. If you're feeling weighed down, do yourself a favor and start tossing whatever you can overboard.

3. MAKE EYE CONTACT

When my kids were little, prior to giving them any sort of instructions, I'd first say to them, "Look at my eyeballs."

For example, I'd say, "Hey, Jameson, look at my eyeballs. We are going to leave the park in just a few minutes, so choose just one more thing to do." Or "Raegan, look at my eyeballs. Go get your shoes on and then get in the car."

Why? Because without eye contact, my instructions would easily get lost in a sea of other things they were doing, thinking, or focusing on. Eye contact ensured they heard me. Apart from when I'm driving, listening to my kids tell me about something that happened at school requires eye contact. I can *hear* them without eye contact, but truly *listening* to them requires eyeballs.

They know I'm listening and actively engaged in the conversation when my face is directed at theirs. I mean, come on. I can't even cut bread without chopping my own finger off. Why would I think I could give my kids the attention they need while multitasking on home chores or editing a book? It just can't be done. I mean, not without some blood loss. Something's always going to end up giving. If you want to be more present for the people in your life, let eye contact do the heavy lifting.

4. PRACTICE THE ART OF COMPARTMENTALIZATION

I'm going to level with you. While I've gotten better at it over the years, compartmentalization is not one of my strengths. If compartmentalizing is the act of mentally setting stressors aside for a period of time, my approach looks more like dumping them all into a kiddie pool and then stewing in them. Sort of like my own DIY spa treatment.

I've always been impressed by people who seem able to push stressors from their mind with ease to get things done. So in recent years, I started asking them about it. I wanted to know exactly *how* they compartmentalize so well. How do they avoid letting concerns and conflicts, whether big or small, distract them from a hard day's work or an afternoon of leisure? What I found was that while yes, compartmentalization may come naturally to some, there's a strategy to it, one we can all learn to implement.

Don't get me wrong: compartmentalization can be a negative coping strategy, especially when it comes to our emotional lives. We can suppress our feelings and ignore triggering circumstances until they start to bubble over in other ways. But for those of us with a tendency to overthink *everything*, compartmentalization can offer us some much needed reprieve.

I took the question to friends, family, and of course, those on Instagram notorious for their stellar compartmentalization skills. This is what they had to say about how they pull it off.

- **Visualize Boxing It Up:** This was by far the most common response. Compartmentalizers envision literally boxing up the issue and sticking it on a shelf. Rebecca says she calls it "shelving."
- **Schedule a Time to Address It in the Future:** This was the second most recommended strategy for compartmentalization. Carolyn says she decides a time (a literal time on the clock) when she can mentally pick it back up again. Katie says, "I visualize it as an appointment/task and 'schedule' it for later." Sara said she "allows time later as

needed to think, process and feel." Maybe it's a large project at work, a phone call that needs to be returned, a conversation with a disgruntled neighbor, a payment that needs to be made, or a plan of care that needs to be developed. Whatever it is, good compartmentalizers decide ahead of time when they're going to deal with it, and then turn back to the present moment until then.

- **Prioritize What Your Brain Needs *Now*:** My friend Nikki is a stellar compartmentalizer. As we chatted in her car about something I couldn't seem to shake, I asked her how she's able to set things aside so well. In summary, this is what she had to say: I remind myself that now is not the time to address the issue. It's easy to take the time we've set aside for rest, play, work, or connection and then waste it stressing about issues we have no control over right now. When we do that, we end up missing out on our chance to fill back up or be productive. Then when it comes time to actually address the issue, we've got nothing left in the tank. I set it aside so I don't miss my chance to recharge.

- **Trust Yourself:** Jane said that she trusts herself "to handle what comes." Think back to the last time one of your concerns came to fruition. What happened? You handled it, and the issue likely wound up being relatively anticlimactic. Often times the things we dread and stress about never come to fruition anyway.

- **Make a List:** Getting it out of your head and down on paper can help you stop ruminating over the things weighing on you.

- **Eat Breakfast:** I love this one. Lisa said compartmentalizing is much easier after breakfast and coffee. Perhaps you aren't actually that stressed. Maybe you're just hangry.

- **Give Yourself Verbal Instructions:** Jackie suggests giving yourself step-by-step instructions to stay on task and in the moment: "You're going to do X. And then you're going to do Y." Saying it out loud can be empowering.

5. FEEL YOUR FEET

Now, I don't mean reach down and literally touch your feet with your hands. This isn't a strategy reserved for the flexible. What I mean is stop and notice the way your feet feel: whether they're on the ground, kicked up on a beach chair, jogging on a treadmill, or pressing on the gas pedal while you listen to this in audiobook format. Wherever you are, take a moment to come back to the present by noticing the feeling of your body against the earth.

When we pay attention to the crunch of the snow as we walk to get the mail, it pulls us into the present. Or when we intentionally feel the steering wheel in our hands as our kids tell us about their day on the way home from school, it helps us pay better attention to the words they are speaking *right now*, rather than the video call we have in an hour or the chicken we forgot to thaw for dinner.

This strategy is known as grounding, and it is meant to reorient you to the here and now. It doesn't just have to be your feet. Just taking a moment to appreciate the wind on your skin can draw you into the present moment.

Much of the difficulty with being present comes from our wandering minds. They trail off to deal with issues we foresee in the future or go back in time to replay events or conversations. There we are at home on a lovely Saturday morning while our heads are stuck back on Wednesday, wishing we'd said something a little less cringey to our coworker.

What I love most about grounding is that it's often followed by gratitude. With a chaotic calendar and distracted mind, there is less room for a grateful heart. Taking a moment to feel your feet can lead you to appreciate the blessings surrounding you.

6. GET OUTDOORS

One of the fastest ways to become more present is to go outside. Time in nature, however brief, has been proven to have a positive impact on your overall well-being and mental health.

Richard Louv, in his bestselling book *Last Child in the Woods*, tells us it's time to stop viewing time spent in nature as leisure time. "Most parents have an acutely tuned sense of responsibility—to the point where they consider relaxation and leisure, for themselves or their children, a self-indulgent luxury," he writes. "By taking nature experiences out of the leisure column and placing it in the health column, we are more likely to take our children on that hike—more likely to, well, have fun. Such a change in outlook is crucial. The stakes are high, and the consequence more evident when children reach their teen years."

Even just being able to *see* nature has a positive impact. Environmental psychologists Stephan and Rachel Kaplan studied more than twelve hundred office workers and found that "those with a window view of trees, bushes or large lawns experience significantly less frustration and more work enthusiasm than those employees without such views." If viewing nature can decrease our frustration and bolster enthusiasm for our work, the effect of actually spending time in nature must be even greater.

As my own work deadline nears, I am tempted to stay indoors and pound away on my keyboard until I have transcribed the words I have in my brain to the pages of this book. Yet more often than not, a change in scenery and some outdoor activity actually helps me pull a more cohesive thought from the words bouncing around my brain. Sometimes we need the kind of change in perspective that only comes from exposure to nature. While it can look like a procrastination technique, setting your work aside to stroll through the woods or even just take a walk around the block can be the most productive thing you do with your time.

There were days, even weeks, when I just couldn't make sense of what I was trying to say in this book. Even when I had words to type, my crazy busy schedule kept me on the move rather than planted at my computer. The longer the writing lull lasted, the more anxious I'd grow—which only served to lengthen said lull. But when I stopped viewing the hours away from my computer as a lack of progress and instead started viewing them as priming the pump, it was so freeing. My mind was at work, spinning out the concepts and applying them to my day-to-day life. Then, when I did sit back down at my computer, my writing time was even more efficient.

Time outdoors begets more time outdoors. Don't be surprised if you find that the more time you spend outside, the more your mind and body will pull you out once again.

7. LEAN INTO THE CRAZY

I think we'd all agree that a two-hour coffee date with a bestie would do a far better job of replenishing our capacity than sitting in the parking lot during that awkward thirty-minute window between kids' practices. But you know what? During busy seasons, beggars can't be choosers. If moments like those are your only opportunities to replenish your capacity, lean into them. Bring a book, listen to an audiobook, or maybe find a park down the road and spend an hour looking for mushrooms. (Just be sure you know what you're looking for. Don't go poisoning yourself on my account. In the words of foraging expert Alexis Nikole, "Happy snacking. Don't die.")

Remember, it's easier to lean into the chaos when that chaos is something you've chosen, on purpose. Once you begin taking back control of your calendar, eliminating hurry, guarding your margin, ruthlessly under-committing, and becoming more proactive with your approach to chaos, the busy seasons aren't only more tolerable; they can even become enjoyable.

Every moment comes with one opportunity to be attentive for it. Distracted moments aren't retrievable. There's no undo button for time. What's done is done. Leaning into the crazy begins by changing the narrative around it and viewing these moments as gifts rather than unfortunate turns of event. Instead of harping on the negative aspects of the chaos, look for the good. Instead of begrudgingly enduring the messy, chaotic, and busier-than-you'd-like periods of time, forage through them to find the delectable moments. Don't be surprised if you end up with an armful of moments that matter—moments you'd never even thought to look for.

TIP FOR BEING BUSY WELL: BYOD (BRING YOUR OWN DOPAMINE)

Dopamine plays a pivotal role in how we function. Unlike serotonin, oxytocin, and endorphins, dopamine is released on anticipation of a reward. Because of that, it helps drive our motivation and desire. When you're overwhelmed by a busy season, a solid source of dopamine can be harder to come by. We get stuck in a survival rut and have very little time for the things that naturally boost our feel-good brain chemicals. When this is the case, it's even more important to get out there and forage for your own dopamine.

Take a ten-minute stroll through the woods. Drink some water or eat a healthy high-protein snack (sometimes we're just dehydrated or hungry). Dip your face in a bowl of ice-cold water. It's basically a less extreme cold plunge, but man, does it wake you up. Foraging, fishing, hunting, and thrifting offer up dopamine because the thrill of the hunt is half the fun. If you only have a few minutes, pop in your earbuds and go for a short but intense run. (Or simply refer to them as "earpods" or "airbuds" in front of your teens and watch them roll their eyes at you. Misusing popular words or slang terms to my kids is sometimes enough of a comical brain boost for me.)

When feeling overwhelmed, distracted, and unsettled, it's far easier to turn to fake-fun activities (like watching television or scrolling through social media) for dopamine. If you find your anxiety rising and motivation waning, it may be time to hunt down some real dopamine.

CHAPTER FOURTEEN

Be Intentional
The Art of Deciding for Yourself

Have you ever worked hard at something, given it your all, and felt proud of your effort—only to realize it had been a total waste of time? You were intentional, thorough, proactive even, but in the end, it turned out that you'd been prioritizing the wrong thing.

When my youngest daughter was just a couple years old, she, like many kids, had experienced so many ear infections that she needed to have tubes put in her ears. During a routine checkup years later, our doctor noticed the hole in one of her ears where the tube had been wasn't healing as quickly as it should have. She referred us to an ear, nose, and throat doctor, who confirmed the diagnosis and recommended we give it a few more months before taking any action. Often, this issue will resolve itself with a little more time. But before we left the appointment, the doctor advised us not to let our daughter submerge her head in water without first securely plugging her ear with wax. *Blerg. It's always something, isn't it?*

Since we spend our summers jumping into lake water, my full-time job became making sure Amelia's right ear canal was properly secured whenever she swam. This proved remarkably more difficult than it sounded. The wax itself held for all of four seconds in the water, so the only way I found to keep it in place was to put a swim cap over her head too. It was a whole thing.

Months passed, the summer concluded, and we followed up with her ENT. "Good news," he said. "The hole in her left ear has healed up nicely."

My eyes widened, and I worked really hard to keep a straight face. *Did he just say* left *ear?* Calmly, I said to him, "I thought it was her right ear."

He checked his notes again and assured me, it had been her left ear all along. This meant I had spent the entire summer intentionally working to plug *the wrong ear*! Every day, multiple times a day even, I'd squeeze wax into her right ear, secure it with a swim cap, and readjust it as needed for absolutely no reason whatsoever. There she was, just bobbing up and down in the lake water with her affected ear exposed to the elements, as her mother diligently worked to keep the wrong ear protected.

We often do this same thing with our time, energy, and attention. We can squander them away on things that may appear on the outside to be an important use of time but are in fact quite the opposite. Overthinking, extensive planning, staying on trend, replicating outdated traditions, maintaining an idealistic image, and even volunteering can all, at first glance, appear to be worthwhile endeavors. However, when you look past the smoke and mirrors, you may find they're just the hurried life disguised as purposeful living.

I'm not telling you to stop volunteering or put a hold on all family traditions. The mitigating factor here is timing. We get into trouble when we completely ignore our current season of life or the challenges we're now facing when making commitments or deciding to continue old ones. Volunteering to lead a small group or book club or to coach youth soccer are wonderful commitments to make. But as I said earlier, just because you've always done it doesn't mean you have to do it for life. As the seasons in your life change, so will the things you're called to participate in. Being busy well means we're careful to be busy about the *right things*.

Another factor to consider when assessing your calendar is your motivation behind the commitment. Is it essential, or are you just trying to keep pace with someone else? Does the club sport schedule actually fit your family's needs during this season, or are you simply afraid your child will be left behind without it? Are you maintaining a leadership role in an organization because it lights you up, or are you struggling to relinquish control to someone else? Participating in something because you "should" may actually be a sign that you shouldn't.

We create busy seasons out of slow ones when we feel compelled to keep commitments that have run their course or maintain roles we simply don't have the capacity for. There is a time to be the leader and a time to show up as a participant. There is a time to join a gym and a time to opt for subdivision strolls. There is a season for slow-cooked, homemade family dinners and a season when dinner means fast food, cereal, or popcorn for the win. The pace becomes a bit irrelevant when we're present and attentive for the life we're living. Let us stop making it harder on ourselves by pouring our heart and soul into the right things at the wrong time.

If you're in a season in which even signing up to bring napkins for the classroom Valentine's Day party is too much, don't beat yourself up over it. Lean into it, harness the power of saying no, and find the pockets of margin available to you. And don't forget to bubblewrap the busy season you're in to ensure a bit of reprieve is on the horizon.

Being in a busy season isn't a bad thing; it just is. We rarely grow completely overwhelmed by just a few weeks of chaos. The sense of overwhelm occurs when busy seasons start to blur together into one long, seemingly endless life of hurry. As Tumnus put it in C. S. Lewis's *The Lion, the Witch, and the Wardrobe*, it's feels like it's "always winter, but never Christmas." It's okay to let the other parents bring in those Valentine's Day party supplies so you stand a chance at catching your breath. Besides, if your children are in elementary school, trust me, there's another class party just around the corner.

Being busy well requires that we capitalize on our slower seasons by maintaining margin. Just because we have the time doesn't mean we need to fill it. When we leave the margin in our calendars instead of compulsively adding in more, we create an opportunity for the rest we need and the spontaneous adventures we long for. In the words of Erica Layne, "Rest is not idle, is not wasteful. Sometimes rest is the most productive thing you can do for the body and soul."

We tell our kids that boredom is good for their brains, but we fail to grant ourselves the same privilege. "Boredom is an opportunity for discovery and invention," writes psychiatrist Anna Lembke in *Dopamine Nation.* "It creates the space necessary for a new thought to form, without which we are endlessly reacting to stimuli around us, rather than allowing ourselves to be within our lived experience."

In a similar way, spending time participating in our favorite activities and hobbies is anything but wasteful. Yet for some reason, leisure seems to be the very last thing we add to our calendars. We try to squeeze it in when we can instead of planning for it with intention. It's become an afterthought in our productivity-addicted world. It's a luxury only afforded to those who've earned it.

Hunting for mushrooms on your day off feels wasteful. Reading a novel instead of getting ahead for the week feels lazy. We've got to flip this script and start looking at it from a different angle. Leaving space for the things that fill us up is the cheat code for living a full life in a too-full world. It's what allows us to enjoy both the slow seasons as well as those busier ones.

But it's up to you to hold that space. Nobody else out there is going to do it for you.

A HOBBY FOR EVERY SEASON

Living in Michigan, we have the luxury of experiencing the height of all four weather seasons, and winter is our longest one. I didn't grow up in a "winter family." Sure, I played outside in the snow as a child, but apart from that we didn't participate in any sort of outdoor winter activities. Once I became an adult, I spent as little time outdoors as possible throughout the winter months. My winter exposure consisted of getting the mail, carrying in the groceries, or briskly walking from the parking lot into work. Every winter, my goal was to survive it. Learning to actually *enjoy* winter never occurred to me.

It wasn't until that cold November morning when I joined my son and his light-up boots to go hunting that I started to question if maybe I hadn't been giving winter a fair shake. Since Jameson had flashlights for feet, we easily navigated our way to the deer blind in the pitch black. Once inside, my dad positioned me in front of a small opening and said: "Just let me know if you see a deer." *Roger that.*

Once situated, I popped in my earbuds and hit play on the audiobook I downloaded for this very occasion. It quickly became apparent, however, that a deer blind really wasn't the place for audiobooks. You need your ears to hear what's going on outside and to acknowledge the whispers from your fellow hunters. So I slipped my earbuds back in my pocket and proceeded to stare into the woods, alert for any sort of activity.

By the time we went home that day, my toes were frozen solid, but the cold, hours of silence had been surprisingly refreshing. We had woken well before dawn, but somehow, I didn't feel the least bit tired. Instead, I felt both invigorated and calmer. Freezing my face off for hours out in nature left me longing for more.

After that, I started dipping those frozen toes of mine into winter every chance I got. I'd bundle up for a long walk outside and jump at the chance to join my dad in his hunting blind as often as I could.

In time, we learned to downhill ski, and I recently started making maple syrup, an outdoor activity reserved for the dead of winter.

I used to live under the theory that winter was meant to be endured, not enjoyed. Now, however, I look forward to winter the same as summer. Sure, it's overcast often. It's not uncommon to go weeks at a time without even seeing the sun in Michigan. But with activities to look forward to peppered throughout this frigid season, I rarely notice the missing sun. I'm too busy getting a participation trophy for all four seasons now.

We can do the same throughout the varying seasons of life as well. Whether you're focused on your career right now, nursing babies, launching young adults into the world, caring for aging parents, welcoming grandbabies, or like me, in the middle of your chauffeur era: soul-filling opportunities await us. You don't have to wait until the season changes to fill back up again. No matter the season you're in, whether calm or chaotic, overwhelming or refreshing, you can create soul-filling habits, carve out pockets of margin, and adopt hobbies that energize you.

If the only rest and leisure time you can muster is fifteen minutes with your nose in a novel before falling asleep, that's okay. Sometimes all you've got time for is an at-home date night with your spouse while your kids eat chicken nuggets in front of a movie. It all counts. The moments that matter don't lose their potency just because you have to be busy right now. If you know what you're looking for and you give them the attention they deserve, those moments will fill you up just the same.

I started to panic the other day while skiing down a hill I had very little business skiing down. It was *steeeep*, but all three of my kids had taken on this black diamond, and I won't let myself get bested by them. Not yet, at least. When I was just a quarter of the way down this hill, I started to grow anxious, realizing I still had so far to go, and it wasn't getting any less steep any time soon. Instead of bailing out and trying to walk down the run, I took a deep breath and said, out loud, like a weirdo, "Just ride what's in front of you, Rachelle!"

I realized my eyes kept darting too far ahead of me. Instead of looking ahead at what was left to tackle, I brought myself back to the moment and started taking it just one turn at a time. Doing so allowed me to better handle the rough terrain and enjoy the ride (best I could, anyway) as it unfolded. Busy seasons can be tackled the same way: one wild turn at a time.

If you tend to keep your eyes ten steps ahead of yourself, I want to encourage you to come back to your mat. Be where you are. Ride the run in front you. Take it one turn at a time so that you're able to enjoy what's available to you in the season you're in.

THE MONETIZATION TEMPTATION

My friend Amy grows flowers and turns them into the most beautiful bouquets. She sells these handcrafted works of art from spring until fall each year. When her flowerbeds stop blooming, she shuts down operations until the next year.

Once, in passing, my husband asked her husband, "Hey, has Amy ever considered building a greenhouse and selling flowers year-round? I bet her business would do really well in the winter if she did."

His response was, "She has thought about it. But have you ever heard the story of the Mexican fisherman?"

He was referring to the parable by German writer Heinrich Boll titled *Anekdote Zur Senkung Der Arbeitsmoral*. Literally translated, means, *Anecdote to Drop the Working Moral*.

Here's my brief adaptation of that very story.

While on vacation in Mexico, a businessman spotted a local man fishing on the shore in a small village. The fisherman had just brought in his haul of freshly caught fish when the businessman asked him how long it had taken to catch them all. The fisherman replied, "Just a few hours."

The businessman, wondering why he doesn't stay out longer to catch even more fish, asked him, "What do you do with the rest of your time?"

The fisherman replied, "I sleep late, fish a little, play with my children, take siestas with my wife, stroll into the village each evening where I sip wine and play guitar with my amigos. I have a full and busy life, señor."

The businessman offered to help this fisherman grow his business, telling him if he worked harder and longer he could catch more fish and make more money. "Eventually," the businessman explained, "You could even hire employees and buy multiple fishing boats to catch even more fish. In time, you could cut out the middleman and sell directly to the processor, or better yet, open your own cannery."

"Then what?" asked the fisherman.

The businessman laughed and said, "That's the best part. When the time is right you could sell your company and make millions!"

"Millions—then what?"

"Well, then you would retire and move to a small coastal fishing village where you would sleep late, fish a little, play with your kids, take siestas with your wife, stroll to the village in the evenings where you could sip wine and play guitar with your amigos . . ."

I love this story. It's such a great reminder to look ahead at what it is we're hoping to achieve before pursuing goals and scheduling things into our calendar. We must protect our capacity and resist the pressure to make our lives unnecessarily complicated.

INFLUENCERS IN THE WILD

It was seven in the morning when my sister and I grabbed a cappuccino and called for a rideshare. Well, seven in the morning in Italy. Our brains were still on US time, so it felt like the middle of the day for us. Since we were already wide awake, we figured: What better time to explore the sites in Rome than before everyone else in town wakes up?

When we arrived at the Fountain of Trevi, though, it was still surprisingly busy. Except it wasn't crowded with tourists but rather influencers.

There were couples and individuals awkwardly posing in front of smartphones on tripods. There were girls dressed in the fanciest attire, their #husbandsofinstagram patiently recording their amateur model moves. The group that stuck out to me most was a family of four accompanied by a camera crew and a stylist. Over and over, they captured the same scene on film. They each tossed a coin over their shoulder into the fountain, turned to each other for high fives, and then embraced one another with huge smiles as if it were the first time.

Except it wasn't. They were repeating the scene, over and over again, until it was perfect. I don't know who these people were or what that footage was for, but there they were, manufacturing a moment and then portraying it as a spontaneous one.

It wasn't just at the Fountain of Trevi. It was everywhere we went. While we waited for a bakery to open in Vernazza, we watched a young couple set up a faux picnic on the wet pier in front of their tripod. It was 7:30 a.m. and nothing was even open. Yet they were out there freezing their buns off on a cool fall morning for a photo op that wasn't even real. The pier in Vernazza is a prime photo-taking spot, and it's typically *covered* in tourists. Nobody is spreading out a whole picnic blanket IRL out there.

There's a temptation these days that other generations never had to deal with: the temptation to monetize our hobbies, build a brand, and showcase every meaningful moment to an audience we'll never meet face to face. Instead of just raising chickens and selling eggs to local friends, we think we've got to start a YouTube channel and sell our new course, "How to Start Raising Chickens." It can begin to feel like every hobby needs to come with a cost analysis spreadsheet describing how you'll earn back your investment.

Let me be clear: there's nothing wrong with monetizing the things you're good at. I'm not knocking your business, big or small. I've got some good friends running successful online businesses. The ability to grow an online business that can give us the income and employment autonomy we desire is a beautiful thing. The trouble is that it's remarkably easy to adopt a new hobby or start a new project and then assume the natural progression is to monetize it. After all, we see it happening all over our social feeds.

What I want to do is flag down those of you who feel pressured to start monetizing your hobby or building a social platform out of your motherhood. You don't have to do it. In fact, I can't help but wonder if decades from now, we'll look back and wonder why we ever did.

Everything comes at a cost. Even this book in your hands comes at a cost to time I could have devoted elsewhere, right? Before feeling pressured into turning your workouts into personal coaching sessions, or teaching online art classes after hours, I want you to consider that parable of the fisherman and ask yourself, "But at what cost? What's my end game?" It's okay to homestead for the sustainability alone. It's okay to start a blog just for fun, to sell your gorgeous flowers only in the summer season, and to take a family vacation without becoming a travel blogger.

It's okay to adopt a hobby that never produces an income. To make elaborate birthday cakes for your kids and never market them to a wider audience. To start a local cookie decorating business you never take national. To bottle your homemade hot sauce or handcrafted syrup just to give away as gifts. To share design advice online because you're good at it without ever pitching HGTV for your own show.

Don't be afraid to keep some things sacred. To protect the things that light you up so they're sure to keep lighting you up. If you're determined to turn a profit doing what you love, by all means, go get it. Just keep in mind that there are careers and then there are hobbies. Don't feel pressured to monetize the joy out of your favorite activities. It's a surefire way to leave you busy about all the wrong things.

WHEN IT ALL MATTERS MOST

Simple living, personal growth, and time-management books often tell us to prioritize the things that matter and eliminate what doesn't. That's all well and good. Nothing clutters up your calendar and reduces your mental load like keeping up with a bunch of things that don't matter.

But what do we do during the seasons when it *all* matters most? When we have aging parents who rely on us, kids who've worked hard to make that team, or a child's gym class head injury that overturns the family calendar? Sometimes the things that matter can be cupped in the palm of one hand. Other times, however, you've got to put your back into it. Minimalism with no kids looks different than minimalism with babies. And they both look different than minimalism with middle and high schoolers. The same goes for your calendar.

There's no way for me to write a paragraph, equation, algorithm, or book to instruct you on which things you should and shouldn't be investing your time, energy, and attention in. To do so would be negligent and arrogant. Instead, as we come to the end of this book, I'll share a few questions I ask myself when making similar decisions in hopes they'll help you decide well when the time comes. Ultimately, though, it starts by first questioning the routes that seem obvious.

"Oh, we're parents; of course we're going to spend our weekends on youth sports." "Oh, we're empty nesters now; of course we're going to say yes to every volunteer opportunity asked of us." Just because the path may be tried and true for someone else doesn't mean it's meant for you.

The first step in making wise choices with our time, energy, and attention is to second guess what's expected. Just because everyone else is doing it, or because you've always done it, or because others expect it of you, doesn't mean it's right for you. It very well may be. But when you start by clearing the expectation slate, you're better able to fill your life with the tasks and activities that really matter.

Once you've set aside expectations, start asking yourself questions like:

- What's my priority in this season?
- What am I building toward?
- What will I be proud of in years to come?
- Do I truly have the capacity for this?
- Am I able to still maintain margin if I take this on?
- Will I still be able to be present for the things I care most about if I do this?

Remember, this is your life. What do you want to pay attention to? Where do you want to allocate your minutes and disperse your capacity? Being busy well isn't about becoming busier, more productive, or even slamming on the brakes. It's a method for living an unhurried life even when your calendar is a mess. It's about cultivating a full life while ensuring you reserve capacity for the moments that matter. Sometimes, though, the things that matter during a given season of life are many, and we're left juggling more than we care to manage. Despite your best efforts to simplify, you may find yourself flat-out forced to carry more than you intended to.

Simplicity, minimalism, and the elimination of the inessential can work wonders to help us carve out the time, energy, and attention we've been lacking. But what do we do when there simply isn't anything left to eliminate? What do we do when we've simplified our calendars and culled the clutter as much as possible but are still facing a load of things to do and places to go? That's when we let our busy protocol step up to the plate, while we go ahead and set more realistic expectations around what intentional living really looks like.

Because despite what you may read, living with intention isn't all 5 a.m. morning routines, ice baths, nomadic living, or off-the-grid homesteading. It's you, taking the time to choose your own adventure and purposefully fill your life with the things you were created to do. Not the things you *should* be doing or have *always* done, but the things meant for you, right now.

Living with intention may land you chauffeuring preteens around the city or snuggling with a couple of kids who have the stomach bug, knowing it's only a matter of time before it comes for you as well. Sometimes living with intention means working overtime to pay off debt or canceling all plans to be there for a friend going through a rough patch. Sure, sometimes there are seasons when your habits and routines get executed with flawless precision. *How to Be Busy* is here to help you experience more of those while holding you up when they start to crumble. Busy doesn't have to define you, but it doesn't have to destroy you either. We can be busy well. We can take on the more hectic seasons strategically, intentionally, and joyfully.

Finally, remember: what we're busy *about* matters as much as how busy we are. When we're busy about the right things, we'll find we have just a little more confidence and capacity to push through, because there is purpose hiding within that chaos.

Whether your intentional life leaves you hiking with your family or driving around the city like you're a full-time bus driver now, the important thing is that you choose it—with intention. That you embrace the season you're in, with all its highs and lows. That you don't let bouts of busyness morph into a frantic lifestyle. Most importantly, that you show up fully and attentively for the life you're living.

That's how we spot the moments that matter in the middle of the mess. That's how we're sure to soak up *these* good ole days as they're unfolding.

Resources

Your Matrix

	Urgent	Not Urgent
Important	**Quadrant I** Urgent and Important	**Quadrant II** Not Urgent but Important
Not Important	**Quadrant III** Urgent but Not Important	**Quadrant IV** Not Urgent and Not Important

Your Brain Dump

TO DO:

TODAY:

DELEGATE:

FOR FUN:

Your Busy Protocol

1 Pause
Halt all new plans.

2 Purge
It's time for a brain dump.

3 Prune
What can you eliminate, simplify, or postpone?

4 Pass Off
What can you delegate?

5 Protect
When does your busy season end? What days, weeks, or season can you bubble wrap?

Acknowledgments

Endless thank you to my husband, Paul. You've been an important part of every one of my seasons thus far. There is nobody else I'd want to venture through the chaos with. Thank you for encouraging me to make the most of it while challenging me toward efficiency and focus. You're the best of both worlds.

To my small partners in crime, Jameson, Raegan, and Amelia. You've made this season of motherhood worth every drop of crazy. I couldn't do the work I do without your support, encouragement, and levity. Thanks for keeping life interesting and ensuring I always have another wild story to write about.

Valerie Weaver-Zercher, it was an honor to work with you again. You knew what this book could become even when it was still foggy for me. Thank you for your trust, support, and incredible skill as an editor. Once again, you made this book better and I'm so grateful for you.

Thank you to the team at Broadleaf Books for all your hard work in bringing this book to life. I'm so grateful for the opportunity, as well as your enthusiasm along the way.

Special thanks to Carolyn Kersten, Courtney Kephart, and Nikki Maggie for wading through the first drafts. It's a tall ask, and you took it on without hesitation. I couldn't have done it without both your brutal honesty and enthusiastic high fives.

To my sisters, Amy, Raeanne, and Renee, thank you for fielding my phone calls, carrying me through the thick of it, and reminding me to finish well. You helped keep me sane throughout this maddening process.

And thank you, thank you, thank you to the Abundant Life With Less community. Thanks to each of you who answered surveys and shared your heart via email or direct messages. This is an actual book because of your support and added insight.

Notes

CHAPTER 3

29 *"feel nourished and refreshed"*: Catherine Price, *The Power of Fun: How to Feel Alive Again* (New York: Dial Press, 2021), 17.

36 *"more time in Quadrant II"*: Steven Covey, *The Seven Habits of Highly Effective People: Powerful Lessons in Personal Change,* rev. ed. (New York: Simon & Schuster, 2020), 175.

CHAPTER 4

40 *"beyond that which is needed"*: Richard Swenson, *Margin: Restoring Emotional, Physical, Financial, and Time Reserves to Overloaded Lives* (Colorado Springs: NavPress, 2004), 69.

45 *"make life easier later?"*: Kendra Adachi, *The Lazy Genius Way: Embrace What Matters Most, Ditch What Doesn't, and Get Stuff Done* (Colorado Springs: WaterBrook, 2021), 48.

CHAPTER 5

55 *"overly optimistic performance scenarios"*: John Rampton, "What Is the Planning Fallacy and How Can You Avoid It?" *Entrepreneur,* May 12, 2020, https://www.entrepreneur.com/living/what-is-the-planning-fallacy-and-how-can-you-avoid-it/350045

CHAPTER 6

64 *"let go of a lot of other things"*: Bob Goff, *Love Does for Kids* (Nashville, TN: Thomas Nelson, 2018), 177, 178.

CHAPTER 9

104 *"The limit for most individuals is four"*: Paul McDougall, "Humans Can Only Think about Four Things at Once, Study Says," *Information Week*, January 29, 2008, https://www.informationweek.com/it-leadership /humans-can-only-think-about-four-things-at-once-study-says

CHAPTER 10

111 *"one wild and precious life"*: Mary Oliver, "The Summer Day," *House of Light* (Boston: Beacon Press, 1990), 60.

114 *144 times a day:* L'Oreal Thompson Payton, "Americans Check Their Phones 144 Times a Day. Here's How to Cut Back," *Fortune*, July 19, 2023, https://fortune.com/well/2023/07/19/how-to-cut-back-screen-time/

116 *"the thrill of anticipation"*: Daniel Z. Lieberman and Michael E. Long, *The Molecule of More: How a Single Chemical in Your Brain Drives Love, Sex, and Creativity—and Will Determine the Fate of the Human Race* (BenBella Books, 2018), 7.

116 *"succumb to its temptations"*: Oliver Burkeman, *Four Thousand Weeks: Time Management for Mortals* (New York: Farrar, Straus and Giroux, 2021), 94.

117 *"well beyond your original purpose"*: Cal Newport, *Digital Minimalism: Choosing a Focused Life in a Noisy World* (New York: Portfolio, 2019), 76.

123 *"what do you want to pay attention to?"*: Catherine Price, *How to Break Up with Your Phone: The 30-Day Plan to Take Back Your Life* (Berkeley: Ten Speed Press, 2018), 167.

CHAPTER 11

128 *only had to endure 500:* Caitlin Johnson, "Cutting Through the Advertising Clutter," *CBS News Sunday*, September 17, 2006, http://tinyurl/yr7pjss4

CHAPTER 12

142 *"just in case"*: Adam Grant, *Originals: How Non-Conformists Move the World* (New York: Viking, 2016), 23.

CHAPTER 13

162 *overall well-being and mental health:* UCDavisHealth, "3 Ways Getting Outside into Nature Helps Improve Your Health," *Cultivating Health,*

May 3, 2023, https://health.ucdavis.edu/blog/cultivating-health/3-ways
-getting-outside-into-nature-helps-improve-your-health/2023/05

162 *"children reach their teen years"*: Richard Louv, *Last Child in the Woods: Saving Our Children from Nature-Deficit Disorder* (Chapel Hill, NC: Algonquin Books, 2008), 120–121. See especially chapter 9.

162 *"employees without such views"*: Louv, *Last Child in the Woods*.

CHAPTER 14

170 *"do for the body and soul"*: Erica Layne, Life on Purpose Movement website, accessed July 19, 2024, https://ericalayne.co/7-ways-to-accept-and
-lean-into-a-season-of-rest/rest-is-not-idle-2/

170 *"be within our lived experience"*: Anna Lembke, *Dopamine Nation: Finding Balance in an Age of Indulgence* (New York: Dutton, 2021), 41.

174 *"play guitar with your amigos . . ."*: One of the places I read this story was in Timothy Ferriss's *The 4-Hour Workweek: Escape 9-5, Live Anywhere, and Join the New Rich* (New York: Harmony, 2007), 252–53.